NOTHING
BUT THE
TRUTH

NOTHING BUT THE TRUTH

A MEMOIR

MARIE HENEIN

SIGNAL

McCLELLAND
& STEWART

Distributed by Penguin Random House Canada Limited, Toronto.

LIBRARY AND ARCHIVES CANADA CATALOGUING IN PUBLICATION
Title: Nothing but the truth / Marie Henein.
Names: Henein, Marie, 1966- author.
Description: Previously published: Toronto: Signal, 2021.
Identifiers: Canadiana 2019016381X | ISBN 9780771039362 (softcover)
Subjects: LCSH: Henein, Marie, 1966- | LCSH: Criminal defense lawyers—
Canada—Biography. | LCSH: Women lawyers—Canada—Biography. |
LCGFT: Autobiographies.
Classification: LCC KE416.H46 A3 2022 | LCC KF345.Z9 H46 2022 kfmod |
DDC 345.71/05044092—dc23

Cover design: Kelly Hill
Cover photograph: © Markian Lozowchuk 2019. All Rights Reserved

Interior photos are courtesy of the author, except those seen on p. 155
(© Henein Hutchison LLP) and p. 191 (© Matt Barnes)

Printed in the United States of America

Published by Signal,
an imprint of McClelland & Stewart,
a division of Penguin Random House Canada Limited,
a Penguin Random House Company

www.penguinrandomhouse.ca

1st Printing

To my children

So that you will know some of who you were.
And who we will become through you.

Come to the edge.
We might fall.
Come to the edge.
It's too high!
COME TO THE EDGE!
And they came,
And he pushed,
And they flew.

—CHRISTOPHER
LOGUE

CONTENTS

Preface   XI

BEGINNINGS

PROLOGUE   I

1   FROM HERE TO THERE   5

2   WHERE ARE YOU *REALLY* FROM?   15

3   TETA   27

4   IT'S ALL ABOUT THE GLITTER   49

5   THE LIQUOR CONTROL BOARD   75

6   HAVE A HOLLY, JOLLY POLYESTER CHRISTMAS   93

7   LOOK AT THE LIGHTS, AREN'T THEY PRETTY?   107

MIDDLES

8   MARIA GOES TO WORK   127

9   DOES ANYBODY KNOW YOU'RE OUT THERE?   155

10   SORRY, NOT SORRY   171

11   TAKE A BREATH   191

AN END, OF SORTS

12   EXCUSE MY DUST   215

13   SHE MAKES A MEAN BEEF STROGANOFF   227

14   HOME   245

15   QUESTIONS MATTER   253

EPILOGUE: I AM NOT A CAT   273

Photo Captions   281

Acknowledgements   285

About the Author   287

PREFACE

I THOUGHT A LOT ABOUT *not* writing this book. For many reasons. The thing that kept troubling me is that the relationship between me and my clients is deeply personal. It can't be anything else when you are navigating a person through one of the most difficult experiences they will ever live through. Because of that, the best parts of my client's stories, the ones I'd like to tell to reveal them and their cases, happen within the confines of our lawyer-client relationship. Ethically, I must keep those confidences; I simply cannot share those moments. And without those moments, I cannot let you feel the fullness of any case. I cannot give you what you need so that you can make up your own mind or ask the real questions. I also did not want to write the usual lawyer's memoir; a book that summarizes my cases with the typical ruminations about each of them feels wholly unnecessary. I've had clients who have chosen to speak or write publicly about their experience in the criminal justice system and others who have decided that this painful chapter is best forgotten. It is their story to tell. And their choice what they wish to do with it, not mine. Anyway, I hate telling "war stories". It's just not in me.

But there are things I wanted to say, about myself, my profession, about the justice system. It seemed to me this is as good a chance as any because there are so many assumptions and misconceptions about all of these things. The only problem with an autobiography, I learned, is that it comes with an uncomfortable amount of introspection and digging around in places I would frankly rather avoid. Even on a good day, I'm not a big fan of self-dissection. I just don't love my own company that much.

Having told my editor and publisher all these unfortunate facts, they still enlisted me to write. I discovered, every time I sat down to write about myself, what came out were the stories of others. The truth is their stories are mine. It is in the telling of their stories that I think you will find some of me. And in the telling of why I do what I do, I hope you come to know me just a little bit more. I can't promise to rationalize or reconcile what must appear to be disparate parts of me and tie them up into a nice, neat bow, but here it goes, my story. The beginning, the middle, and an end, of sorts.

BEGINNINGS

PROLOGUE

I HAVE A PHOTOGRAPH of one of our family dinners at
my grandmother's house in Toronto. I was five years old.
Weekly family dinners at my Teta's were mandatory, and, as
usual, after dinner my cousins escaped to the basement to
play. Not me. I always preferred the company of the adults.
Every one of these gatherings ended the same way, with
anise-laden arak, our traditional drink, being brought out

from my grandmother's mahogany cabinet. I would watch the adults' sorcery as they mixed the clear liquid with water, turning it into a cloudy white elixir. By the time the sweet licorice-scented smoke from the arak and the cigarettes had settled over the room, the Arabic dancing would begin. Later on, the pounding, joyful rhythm of the Egyptian tablah would give way to the melancholic tones of the famous singers Oum Kalsoum and Fairouz, enveloping everyone in arak-infused homesickness. But it was early yet.

In the picture, my dad is standing in the centre of the group of adults who are lounging on garish velvet furniture. He is in his element, smiling, his arms outstretched, one leg crossed over the other, in mid-dance. It was his signature move, hips swaying, his fingers snapping, a bastardized mash-up of the Lebanese dabka. The women would later chime in with belly dancing. But at that moment, my father had the floor.

I am caught by the camera standing off to the side, arms crossed, wearing checked flammable polyester pants—an immigrant staple—looking straight ahead with a very disapproving look. I have a lousy memory for most things from my childhood, but it's funny that I still feel this moment. And it's where I need to begin. I remember exactly why I had that look on my face. This silliness. Wasted time. How could my father blithely dance with that grin? It was the frivolity of the adults, especially my father, that upset me.

Even at that young age, I was serious. A chronic condition. And while I was given to excess in all sorts of other ways, the emotional frivolity, the sheer happiness of my dad at that moment, pissed me off. I have never, not once, felt what he did. Don't get me wrong—I've had fun. I'm capable of it. But *that* sort of fun, never. There were other things to be done, serious things. And the adults should have had the decency, *my father* should have had the decency, to at least agonize about some of what was being left undone and unsaid while he danced away. But there he was, wildly dancing. *Enjoying* himself. If I had centre stage, I would say things. Not dance.

My mom knows. She tried to console me. As she hugged me to safety tight to her side, she whispered in my ear, as she would throughout my life, *It's never easy, it's never easy for you.* It never is. It's just differing degrees of unease for each of us.

Discomfort is a home of sorts to me. I know it, and find myself restless and searching for it the moment I feel myself slipping into any state of ease. The truth is that I feel most acutely when I have pushed into some state of discomfort. For years, I just thought I liked the exhilaration of the new. But that's not it. It is the unease, the challenge of discomfort, that feels stabilizing. Maybe that is what upset me in that moment. Why wasn't my father feeling that? Why weren't any of them? Did they think that because we had crossed the ocean but held on a little to our dabka and our arak, it was done? That we were *here*?

The truth is, I am still that little girl—this is no transformation story. I've gotten a little taller, but at my core, I am still that serious five-year-old immigrant girl, looking in, the discomfort always scratching beneath my skin, the sounds of Oum Kalsoum and Fairouz, the voices of my home, forever humming in the back of my head.

1

FROM HERE TO THERE

TO HEAR MY PARENTS TELL IT, the life of a Cairene in the mid-twentieth century was bucolic. I hadn't been born yet, of course, but that's how my parents like to recount their life in Egypt. Much of what I know about this, my family history, has been pieced together from fragments of stories that my mother and father have told me over the years. Or the stories that my Teta ("grandmother" in Arabic) would tell me while she made pita and *lahmajeen* in the early mornings as I sat at her kitchen table. Or the fading memories of Gedo, my grandfather, that would trickle out while he was sitting in his wood-panelled family room, blasting a crackly Arabic station on an old portable radio that he had rigged up through a makeshift antenna—anything to get scraps of news from home. Gedo would tell me about how, upon meeting my beautiful grandmother while she was visiting Cairo, he persuaded her to leave her conservative family in Jerusalem and move with him to Egypt. Her Palestinian mother, an austere and uncompromising woman with nine children, warned my Teta that she was going to a very dangerous land with a motorcycle-riding rogue and would probably be killed . . . or worse. Teta went anyway. She could hardly wait to escape to cosmopolitan Cairo.

As Gedo spoke, he would take down the small marble pyramid that he kept on the brick fireplace mantel in his sub-urban Toronto house and hand it to me as though he were taking me on a tour of the actual pyramids. The pale yellow pyramid that I would hold in the palm of my hand was a reminder of home that a family member had brought back from Khan el-Khalili, the souk in Cairo. It was at the base of one of these pyramids, Gedo would tell me, that he and my grandmother stole their first kiss during a sandstorm. It sounded so perfectly romantic.

These stories made me desperate to go to Egypt and see the pyramids and the beaches of Alexandria where my mother and her family vacationed in the summer—to touch things I had been told about, to make sure they were there, that my history was real. There was a time that I decided being a tour guide in Cairo could bring me closer. I warned my mother that I planned on eventually disappearing into the desert with the Bedouins, convinced that these dark nomads had to be my people. Maybe it was because of my endless restlessness, or that Bedouin women were so dark like me, with intricately tattooed hands and faces that I found beautiful. But mostly, it was their eyes, thickly ringed by black kohl, staring out from their weather-beaten faces, eyes that were defiant and proud. That is what I saw and why I kept looking.

After the Bedouins, it was the pharaohs that I obsessed about. I lost count of how many distant relatives visiting from Cairo would bring us drawings of pharaohs on *real* papyrus, presenting them with a preciousness as though they had just been unearthed from Tutankhamen's tomb. *A little piece of home*, they would say about this bit of fakery. For a while in elementary school, I could rhyme off many of the pharaonic dynasties and their kings. I would take out these papyrus drawings, wondering if I looked like Nefertiti or Cleopatra. Were these my people? No, according to my mother, who brought that genealogical delusion to a screeching halt. It was the Egyptian Copts that were descendants of the pharaohs, she announced, not us. We are Lebanese Maronites. I stopped looking at the papyrus pharaohs, chintzy reminders of a history that was never mine.

Evelyn, my mother, had an urban upbringing in the middle of bustling Cairo, although I am sure she is convinced that she is a blue-blooded European. My dad would always call her "the Downtowner." Whenever I would complain about our oppressive suburban existence, Dad would say, "A Downtowner, just like your mother"—not with admiration, but with a mix of exasperation and bewilderment that I could be so dismissive of the magnificence of suburbia, where everything was brand spanking new.

New. That was the point of North America. Newness that you could smell and be a part of. Hope and newness was a heady mix for my immigrant parents, having lived in a country full of thousand-year-old artifacts displayed in dilapidated dusty museums. None of that was ancestral grounding for them or the stuff of rich history or even a source of pride. Those aging, broken ruins of pharaonic times were evidence of cultural decline—*their* culture's decline—and emblematic of a chronic lack of progress. They were ashamed of it, of the oldness of it.

True to my father's nickname, my mother is an urbanite through and through, which I think is why she was finally able to find comfort settling in Toronto. I was going to say where she was finally able to take root, but that is not right; she never did put down deep roots here. To be honest, it was only recently that I started to myself.

For Mom, downtown was the heart of Cairo, where she grew up. She still talks wistfully about going to the outdoor theatre on weekends and watching American movies, from John Wayne westerns to the Cecil B. DeMille epics to any musical on offer: *Gigi*, *Seven Brides for Seven Brothers*, *My Fair Lady*. My parents still love all the glamorous old Hollywood stars. Mom so desperately wanted to be one of those seemingly liberated actresses, going so far as to model her look in Cairo after what she saw in those American movies. If you saw my mother back then, you would swear that she had just stepped out of *Breakfast at Tiffany's*. An Egyptian Audrey Hepburn, lithe, beautiful and aloof. She had angular features and rather light skin for an Egyptian woman. She was rail thin in a place where a premium was put on voluptuousness. I have a photo of her with her brothers on the beach in Alexandria. She is sitting on the sand, staring glamorously at the camera in her leopard-print capris and cat-eye glasses. Smiling but looking like she didn't quite belong. Mom often proudly tells me that she would spend days combing through the markets with her mother, my Teta, and her youngest brother, Sami, looking for fabric or just the right crystal beads to knock off a dress that she had seen in a movie. She describes the colours of her dresses, the beautiful imported fabrics, the crepe de Chine and the tulle, the shoes dyed to perfectly match the dress, and then she stops herself. Surrounding a boy with that many sequins. "I shouldn't have made Sami spend so much time shopping with me," she sometimes says, but only when she goes looking for answers. Then she remembers, corrects herself. No, that can't be right. Sami was perfect.

My father, Joseph, is of Lebanese origin but Cairo-born. For the longest time, he was proud that he belonged to Egypt, a polar opposite of my mother in every way. He is short but acts as though he is six feet tall. He is a big personality who ended up spending his life stuck in the wrong profession. He'd wanted to be a lawyer, but in Egypt, being a lawyer was a useless profession and a familial embarrassment—no one could afford them. "What do you want to do being a lawyer?" his father would ask him. "Spend your life sitting at the cafés drinking *qahwa*?" (a dense, sludgy Turkish coffee).

My dad would have loved nothing better than to spend his life sitting at cafés drinking and smoking and debating politics. But his family needed money, and his mother, whom he adored, desperately wanted to have a respectable, educated

child, the definitive marker of parental success in Egypt, so off
he went to medical school. But after a week of hanging out with
cadavers, he realized that they were not good conversationalists.
He preferred the company of the living. (My mom, on the other
hand, who has taken decades to acclimatize to the Henein habit
of incessantly talking, would have found them to be perfect conversationalists.) Dad switched to pharmacy, the next best thing
to medical school, and would end up spending fifty years contained behind a dispensary chatting with customers and debating politics. It wasn't a café in Cairo but, being the eternal
optimist that he is, it was the best he could do. I wouldn't learn
about his dream of being a lawyer until I was well on the way
to becoming one myself. He did not impose his dream on me;
I found it by myself. But surely this history, *his* history, must
have been unconsciously nudging me along.

My father grew up in Heliopolis, a suburb of Cairo. Every time he mentions Heliopolis, my family is given the very same etymological lesson. "*Helios*," he always announces as though for the first time, "means 'sun.' *Polis* means 'city.' 'City of the Sun.'" Even my own children recite it with him. "City of the Sun," he repeats, slightly exasperated at our linguistic limitations. "The Unilinguals," he calls us. *The Downtowners. The Unilinguals.* He has an affection for one-word nomenclature, as though his immediate family are a foreign species that need classification. Some days I am a Unilingual and other days I am a Downtowner. I get it. He is a multilingual suburbanite often completely baffled by his own family's alien leanings: my brother Peter's decidedly artistic bent (he was a standup comic for years) and my mother's and my obsession with anything urban. None of it made any sense to him, an upbeat suburban Cairene who loved his life back home.

Dad was the second youngest in a family of three boys and one girl. Recounting stories of his life in Cairo was part of every Sunday afternoon when I was young. They seemed magical, and free and, yes, sometimes fantastical. His escapades in the streets of Heliopolis—the bully who refused to let him walk to school in his early grades, the fights, how his brothers would stand up for him, the silly childhood pranks, and his catalogue of larger-than-life friends who were philosophers, newspaper editors, artists and poets. His friends meant everything. These were his people. Nights were spent at bars and cafés, smoking and drinking until four in the morning. He is wistful for those days in Cairo. He left more behind than my mother. That used to make me angry, but I think I am beginning to understand why some of him wasn't in Canada. Understanding regret must come with age, or maybe we've collected so much of our own by the time we are older that it just becomes easier to sort through someone else's.

Then President Nasser came to power and the life that my parents knew began to fade.

This isn't a history lesson, but I have to confess it is a bit of one for me. When my parents talk about the decision to leave Egypt, they describe the gradual erosion of the country they knew and loved. I was never told of the promise of Nasser, what it was that brought him to power in 1954. While some academics describe him as progressive and visionary, that was not how it felt to my mother and father. They did try to adjust to the new order, but it wasn't easy for cosmopolitan, French-speaking Christians. Nasser was one of the architects of the anti-westernization movement, and during his rule, anti-Semitic and anti-Christian sentiment in Egypt flourished. Europeans and Egyptian Jews, many of whom were expelled, began to leave in droves. My parents' non-Egyptian friends were literally packing up and disappearing overnight.

Gedo's trucking business was taxed into bankruptcy under Nasser's new nationalizing program. My parents had no one to speak French with. What they didn't feel, until it was too late, was the political undercurrent in the country. The Muslim Brotherhood, responding to the poor who had been impoverished by feudalism, were gaining popularity with their message of nationalism and the protection of Islamic values. And as the political current revitalized and empowered the concept of the new Egyptian identity, my parents saw their own Egyptian identity slipping away. They became outsiders. A girl dressed like Audrey Hepburn had nowhere to go in the streets of Cairo; a young, blue-eyed Christian Egyptian man increasingly began to feel that he had no place at those cafés anymore. *You are not a real Egyptian*, my father started hearing. *I'm more Egyptian than you*, he would reply. My father still gets angry, his voice shakes with hurt every time he recounts those conversations. For him, it is the moment he lost his home. I do not know whether it was the card he had to carry identifying him as a Christian or the colour of his eyes betraying his Lebanese heritage, but whatever he was, he was not Nasser's Egyptian. The need to look elsewhere for a home was growing.

We try to find ourselves in the history of others. I have. The stories come out in small spurts, a little bit here, a little bit there, over dinner, during a shopping trip to a Middle Eastern grocery store, in the early morning while Teta was baking *lahmajeen*, or while Dad and Mom were sitting in the family room quietly talking at the end of a day's work. I guess my history was always there—as it is for many of us. I obviously remember some of it. But more recently, my own memories seem to come in fits and starts. I am beginning to realize that the people who held these moments, who kept them for me, are fading one by one. Teta. Gedo. Sami. Maybe that is why these days I am remembering more acutely, or perhaps more desperately. And writing it down. But for many years, I did not.

I wish I could tell you that the back-and-forth of my earliest years of life—the transcontinental shuttling from Cairo to Vancouver to Lebanon to Toronto to Lebanon again and back to Toronto—was seared so clearly in my memory, that somehow all of that consciously became a part of who I am today, that this history, *their* history, formed me. I know now that it did.

These stories—these first steps—are ones I've been told about. That it was the first time my twenty-four-year-old mother had ever been on a plane, that she ran out of food for me, that on this first trip to Canada I apparently rolled off the airline seat. My mother was convinced I had somehow been stolen from the plane in mid-flight until I was found sleeping soundly on the floor under a blanket. Or that my father, desperate to support his young family, would sit at our small kitchen table studying for his pharmacy equivalency exam while Mom and I huddled in our small apartment's one bedroom watching a Hollywood musical. I learn about the loss of the life my parents had growing up and their increased isolation from their own country during a rainy car ride to buy molokhia (an awful leafy green) from Molokhia Mary, an Egyptian transplant whose molokhia farming business never quite took off. I was all of four years old by the time most of that was said and done and we'd finally settled in Toronto.

My parents laugh now about these stories of our first years in this country, disconnected from them in their old age as though they were someone else's, and they are somewhat bewildered by my interest. "Why don't you write something nice," my mom says. "Tell people how well we have done through you. That's a nicer story." "That's a very short book, Mom," I say. We have this conversation over and over again, every time I ask them to tell me a little more. I will tell it, I say, the immigrant-makes-good story, the story that you came to this country to conceive. But I need to have these fragments first, before they are lost to me.

My parents relent and start to tell me.

2

WHERE ARE YOU *REALLY* FROM?

FOR YEARS, AS I MOVED through the streets of this
country, convinced that no one actually knew I was not
born here, as soon as I settled in the back seat of some taxi,
the driver would always ask me that question: "Where are
you from?" And when I answered that I was from here, he
would say, "No no no, where are you *really* from?" There is
no right answer.

For immigrants, we wear this otherness on our face, in our accents, in our tentativeness. It is a speed bump that slows us down just a little bit. We can't take off weightlessly. There is always something tugging at our foot, pulling us back down to earth. We are weighed down just enough to jar us back into line, lest we forget our place. It is a misplaced fear, because we never forget, and we don't need cab drivers to tell us. We know. The dark eyes. The dark hair. The parents with accents. The strange foods we eat. All of it says *you are not from here*.

Even when we think we have shed that, something happens to remind us. Days after 9/11, on the eve of my father's seventieth birthday, I know his family members can't come from Egypt to celebrate with him. The trip will not be easy; they will not be welcome. "Can I get into New York anymore, you think?" I ask my husband. "Why not?" he says. He forgets sometimes. My passport. It says where I'm from. With travel bans, routine borders become a little more nerve-racking for a while. But then we forget again, until a terrorist attack by people with our skin colour. And magically, we see ourselves everywhere because now the new Hollywood villain is usually one of us. That is what they think of our kind. And when I sit in the darkness of the theatre translating the bad guy's Arabic to English for my husband, I am in the back of that cab all over again. Where are you *really* from? *Not here.*

The first time my parents crossed the ocean in 1965, leaving their home behind, it was to move from Cairo to Vancouver. They had applied to immigrate to various countries and were accepted by three: Brazil, Australia, and Canada. My mother had an uncle on her father's side who had settled in Vancouver, so it made the most sense to go there. He told my parents that the country was wonderful, lush, and full of opportunity. The pictures of him showing a colourful backyard and big cars, proved it. So off my parents went. Given the Egyptian government's rules about removing money from the country, my dad could leave with only about $240. He had given a Saudi friend my mother's jewellery and a few thousand dollars for safekeeping and hoped that if he needed it quickly, his friend could find a way to send it over. At the Cairo airport, the guards demanded that all of my parents' luggage be emptied out on the floor— a parting shot, an informal tax, for those having the audacity to leave the "new" Egypt. Most of what my parents had was taken. My mom, who is private and dignified, told me about seeing the few precious wedding gifts she had hoped to save strewn on the ground for everyone to see, including the small marble box with a hand-painted cover that Gedo had given her as an engagement present. He was not an expressive man, and giving her that marble box is one of the few things he said to her. It still upsets her because she has so little left of him now. Between the stopover in London and the need to buy food and diapers, by the time we arrived in Vancouver, my parents had little more than a hundred dollars left.

Vancouver's East End wasn't as it had been sold to us. My mother's uncle was unemployed, drinking, and every day bemoaned leaving his beloved Egypt. After only about four months, we moved out to our own two-bedroom apartment for $200 a month. My father, as he would do many times, swung into high-provider mode. His powers of oration can convince anyone of anything. My hustle comes squarely from him. He contacted the College of Pharmacists (then the

Pharmaceutical Association of British Columbia) to get his licence but was told that no one was available during the summer months to assess his Egyptian university qualifications. Not one to be denied so easily, he decided to go to the college itself, where he found a woman in some administrative office with a sympathetic ear. He explained that he had just arrived from Egypt with no money, a wife and baby daughter to support, and needed to work. She took pity on him and contacted a professor at the University of British Columbia, who agreed to meet with him. Not surprisingly, the college had never had to qualify an Egyptian pharmacist before. My father had all the details of his courses, and the professor pulled an emergency group together to assess his qualifications. He was approved to apprentice, and before he left, the college had found my father a position to fill while he completed his equivalency exams. He was working within the week, earning $1.90 an hour.

Remembering this professor, my dad gets emotional. I'm not sure if it's the vividness of the desperation he felt at that time or that this professor had helped a young Egyptian pharmacist with no job, no contacts, and no money. Maybe it's both. I wanted to verify this piece of history, so I went looking for this man. I found his picture—looking sternly off into the distance while holding a model molecule. John (Jack) Edward Halliday: born in England, he became a professor of pharmacology at the University of British Columbia in 1949 and a professor emeritus in 1977. I hope his family knows that there is one Egyptian pharmacist who has told the story of that spring meeting to his daughter over and over again.

While my dad was busy working as an apprentice and trying to qualify for his licence, my mother was stuck with me in a small apartment in a foreign country with no one to talk to and hardly any English. After a few months, she had developed a chronic body rash—the doctor diagnosed her with stress. With my father's salary and the remaining money being sent from Saudi Arabia, they were just able to afford the rent on the new place. Things didn't improve, though. My mother felt completely at a loss, taking buses to try to make her way around the city but not being able to navigate to where she wanted to go. She carried me everywhere, afraid to let go. After months of this, she returned to the doctor because of her newest ailment, back pains. He suggested the practical solution of putting her very chubby baby down. But she wouldn't let go of me. So off she went, riding up and down on the buses, hanging on to me.

During this time, Gedo left Cairo to find work. He went to Lebanon, on the pretext of a visit, never to return to his home, abandoning what was left of his trucking business and most of the family's possessions. My grandmother and my three uncles joined him shortly afterwards. But my uncles couldn't find jobs, and so all five of them left everything in Lebanon, came to Vancouver and moved into our small apartment.

Being with family again did nothing to cure my mother's rash. Transition did not take. My mother, all of twenty-four years old, continued to spend her days riding up and down the bus line on Robson Street. There was unrelenting rain, each and every day, weather she was not used to. We are sun-dwellers and thrive in light. My mother had gone from her sunny home to a white city with grey weather. She still tells me that every time she got on the bus with me, people would comment on her dark-eyed, brown-headed baby. I was *exotic*. I still hate that word. It means "foreigner" to me.

Mom's family didn't fare any better than her uncle had. Neither my grandfather nor my uncles could find work. Teta and Mom spent their days walking to the end of our street, sitting on the bench, then coming home. When I ask my mother about Vancouver's natural beauty—the mountains and the ocean, the impossibly large flowers that look like they are on steroids—she is surprised and tells me she didn't see any of it. "It wasn't there when I lived in Vancouver," she says. It all was, of course, right outside the door, patiently waiting for her to look up. But she didn't. It was too early.

My mom couldn't acclimatize to this new land, and so after about nine months, my parents and my mother's family decided to leave Canada for good. They packed everything up and returned to their ancestral homeland, Lebanon.

If you have ever spoken to a Lebanese person, you know that the first thing they will tell you is that Beirut was "the Paris of the Middle East." Lebanon is a small country sandwiched between the greenest mountains and the bluest Mediterranean.

My mother to this day wistfully talks about dining on the salty fish pulled fresh from the ocean and then going for a drive through the mountains full of cedars and pistachio trees. You could hear the pistachio nuts popping open on the trees, she tells me. I didn't believe her at first, but it is true—pistachios can and do. This was all before the never-ending war—before Beirut was ripped apart—when the scent of cedars was replaced with the smell of smoke and mortar fire. It was the old Lebanon that my family had wanted to return to. But it was no longer the home they thought they would find. The undercurrent of political tension had begun to erode all of that. My dad could sense it in the air and he began to feel uneasy.

Ever the optimist, though, my dad once again looked for a job. He already had Lebanese citizenship because his father, Emile, had had the foresight to register him with the Lebanese consulate in Egypt. Emile was a small imp of a man with sparkling eyes like my father. I met him a couple of times when he came to stay with us in Toronto and he schooled me in cards, beating me every time. A charming rogue, a hustler through and through, he spoke English perfectly and was a wickedly intelligent man. But as charming as he was, he was also extremely tough and domineering. He came from a well-off Lebanese family, and on his father's death he inherited an apartment building when numerous properties were divided among the many children. His building burned down. Or was mismanaged. Or gambled away. The story seems to change every time I ask. While his siblings prospered, Emile did not. He never held a particularly steady job. There was some un-explained two-year stint in a Saudi or Libyan prison when my father worked to support his mother. I am told that the incarceration was politically motivated, but the lawyer in me doesn't buy that story because he quite simply was not a political activist or at all engaged in political life. The reason too changes every time I ask, and most recently my father has taken to claiming the story was about my grandfather's cousin, not my grandfather. Why I would ever be told any story about my grandfather's cousin defies explanation. The lawyer in me, again. I've given up trying to get to the bottom of it.

My grandfather married my grandmother, Shafika, when she was only fourteen, not uncommon in the Middle East at the time. My father has always kept a picture of his mother at his bedside and he would kiss it before he went to bed and when he woke up. He looks like her—he has the same turquoise eyes. I am told my grandmother was sweet and unnaturally kind, taking strangers into her house to feed and care for. My father would tell me that it was not unusual to come home and find people he didn't know at the dinner table. I think to myself, Is this true? Is this an imagined person, some beatific, unreal charitable creature? I know nothing else about her—who she was, how she felt, what she had hoped for. Years after her death, my father would run into people who would tell him stories about his mother: how she had cooked for them for years, how she had secretly helped their families or had taken care of their children without telling a soul. Even my mother, who did not know her mother-in-law, would hear stories from different sources about this unusually kind woman. This is who she was.

My grandmother died at fifty of a heart attack. One night she woke up while travelling with my father and aunt, called to my dad, and asked him to hold her. He held her to his chest and she died in his arms. My father has told me of this moment many times. I will admit—and this is awful—I never believed him because my dad is a brilliant storyteller and this sounded like a made-up story from a Hollywood movie, the moment where the mother calls out to her favorite son on her deathbed. That is, until recently, when my aunt was visiting, and I subtly cross-examined her. She told me the very same story.

The truth is there, and maybe I should just give up scratching at it.

When my parents arrived in Lebanon, my maternal grandfather was waiting for them. Gedo insisted that they put whatever savings they had left into a bank, which my father did—in the most well-known banking institution in the country. The very next day, the bank declared bankruptcy and we lost everything. That same day, my father bumped into a friend who had worked for Hoechst Pharmaceuticals in Egypt. My father had worked for this company in Cairo, but while he was waiting for a promotion, the Ministry of Labour announced that only Muslims could hold high positions. In Lebanon, though, Hoechst followed different rules. The majority of the company ownership had to be in the name of a Lebanese national. My dad was a perfect choice: personable, hardworking and, most important, Lebanese. In Beirut, being a Christian was not a bar to a promotion.

Dad was soon doing well—well enough to rent a large apartment and boot around town in the company car, a grey Volkswagen Bug. I think being in sales was probably the most fun my father ever had. My mother complains that all he did was drive around and talk all day. Mom has clear lines between respectable and non-respectable jobs. Arabs in general do. In

Egypt, there are only three respectable professions—doctor, pharmacist, and engineer. All other jobs fail to meet this arbitrary respectability threshold. Talking all day in sales is in the non-respectable category. Of course my dad sees it differently. There is nobility and purpose in talking and persuading, something personally invigorating. "I sort of do the same thing Dad did," I say to my mother. "It's different," she says dismissively. I'm not so sure.

Notwithstanding their Lebanese heritage, getting citizenship in Lebanon proved to be impossible for my mother's family. They had let their Lebanese citizenship lapse and in that political environment, they were not able to get the necessary documents. My grandfather and my mother's oldest brother moved to Libya to try to find jobs. By this time, my Palestinian grandmother's family had moved from Jordan to Toronto, and my mother's family, after being unable to establish themselves in Lebanon, had given up and made a second trip across the ocean, also to Toronto. My mother was again left alone, without her immediate family. After seven months, she could not bear it, particularly being away from her mother, so in 1968 she decided to take me on an extended visit to her family in Toronto. Teta, Gedo, and my uncles were living in a neighbourhood called Parkdale. And so, just like that, we moved in and lived with them in their small apartment on Jameson Avenue. My father, having been uprooted so many times, refused to leave Lebanon.

For my mother, this time was different. I have a feeling the move, the separation, was supposed to be permanent. I'm not convinced she ever intended to go back. In Toronto, my mother found a home—she loved the multicultural atmosphere, the way the city buzzed and moved. With her English improving, she was able to get her very first job at the Bank of Nova Scotia not far from where we lived. As she had in Vancouver, she would ride the bus every day, but on these bus rides she found something new: her freedom. She began to breathe, in that way you breathe when you've spent your entire life not being allowed to go out without being escorted by your brothers or parents, to socialize alone, to think of your future as an independent person. She had always belonged to her family or husband or both. She had never been allowed to do what she wanted to do. But now, for the first time, she could go where she wished, unencumbered. No restrictions. Even if she only went as far as a short bus ride to work at the bank, it was something. When she tells me about those days, she speaks of her freedom.

But it was short-lived. Teta was having none of it. Soon, every time my mother wanted to go out, Teta would insist that she take me with her. She refused to babysit or to let my mother socialize alone, even with friends. Raising a daughter without a father was unacceptable to Teta. Family was everything. And so, just as the air had filled my mother's lungs, it began to be slowly sucked out. She could not see a way to make a life here alone, without the support of her family, and on a bank teller's salary. She tells me, "It was this prison or the other." In my culture, women have only two options: their family or their husband. After just shy of a year, the two of us returned to Lebanon to be with my father. A failed liberation that she would never attempt again. But she would save it for me.

During that time we were alone in Toronto, my father didn't talk to my mother. I forgot who he was. Children forget quickly—self-preservation in its crudest form. For years, I was angry at him—how he could let us go that easily, without a fight, without so much as a phone call. But I understand more now. He had uprooted himself repeatedly at my mother's whim and he could not do it one more time. But he would.

While we were in Toronto, the president of Lebanon, Camille Chamoun, a Maronite, was shot in the face. It was not the first assassination attempt, and again he managed to survive. The day of this attempted assassination, my father was working in al-Hamra, Beirut's commercial district. As a result of the assassination attempt, my dad's office closed and everyone was sent home. With roads closed and identity checkpoints manned by armed militia, what was normally a fifteen-minute drive took my father three hours. By the time he got home, his nerves were frayed. He could feel the country erupting. In that moment, my father decided he could no longer live in Lebanon. He spoke to his father, Emile, who told him that he had to leave, that the country was not safe.

The day my mom and I arrived in Lebanon, thinking that we were settling down at last, my father took us to Al Sakhra, a restaurant perched on the cliffs overlooking the Mediterranean, so that my mother could taste the Mediterranean fish she longs for to this day. And while I was trying to figure out who this man was, my dad said he had a surprise for us. We were leaving the Middle East for good.

We were moving to Toronto.

3

TETA

WHEN I TRY TO REMEMBER my early years in Toronto, they play out in vignettes. There is no continuity, no story with a beginning, middle, and end that captures what it felt like when we were trying to get our footing in this new country.

I want to tell you what it feels like—the urgency, the trepidation. How my grandparents, having spent their formative years and every significant moment of their lives in a different country, now feel completely foreign, engulfed by a language and culture that are incomprehensible to them, yet they hang on, year after year, convinced that this is one necessary, difficult step to progress. How my father and mother look forward to just trying to get grounded and make a better life for themselves and their children. *Head down, work hard. The children will make good.* That is where their worth comes from. And how we, the youngest, my cousins and I, want so desperately to integrate, to soak up everything that our new country offers, to be real *Amerikani*, but we have no guidance and more than a little resistance from our parents, who cannot even now let go of their home, their customs, themselves. We are all submerged, my parents, grandparents, uncles, cousins, me. Floating around, buoyed by I don't know what. But we don't drown. Something keeps pushing us back to the surface. Maybe the hope of *better* or *more* or *new*, just around the corner.

I remember things here and there. Playing in the basement with my cousins after our weekly family dinners. Dancing with my uncle Sami to the newest Donna Summer album in training for my fabulous Studio 54 debut. The multi-car family treks to Niagara Falls. What is it I am trying to say to you? Then I know. It is her: Teta was always there. Everything about me in those early years, she was the centre of it all, hanging on to us, grounding us so we didn't drown, quietly pushing us back to the surface again and again. Beginning in this country is her story as much as it is mine.

My grandmother, Nour, which means "light" in Arabic, was born and raised in Jerusalem, the oldest of her many siblings.

I don't know much about her childhood and she never really talked about it. Not because it was traumatic, but because it was in the past. Self-analysis and navel gazing weren't her thing. So many of my friends' parents who come from another country don't like to talk about their histories. Many came here, after all, to forget.

My mother has told me a little bit, that Teta's father worked odd jobs in the local church, and he was neither a great supporter nor, it appears, a particularly loyal husband, although he did show up enough times to give my great-grandmother nine children. Teta's mother, Victoria, was a powerful presence in her children's lives. She ruled the roost. She had to, since there was no one around to help her. I've been told she had a difficult up-bringing. When her father died, my great-grandmother was forcibly taken from her mother by her father's parents and placed in some type of orphanage, where she grew up. She was educated to read and write, a privilege that she did not think to extend to my Teta. She reconciled with her mother later in her life and they were inseparable, but other than that, I don't know any more about her. She was an austere woman. Queen Victoria was warm and fuzzy compared with Teta Vicky.

By the time I met my great-grandmother, when she moved to Canada, she was frail and virtually blind. I remember during our first meeting, she ordered me to sit close to her. When I did, she gripped my arms like a vice as she felt up and down, squeezing my arms and legs, before finally announcing to my mother that I was ready: I had sufficient meat on my bones to be marriageable. She demanded to know what my mother was doing about arranging a marriage for me. My mother's only aspiration for me was that I be educated and financially independent, so this question was not well received.

She demurred with a simple "Not for *my* daughter"—the emphasis signalling that I did not belong to them. My mother did that a lot—laid claim to me. She did everything to shield me from the shackles of my culture. I was *her* daughter, not Egypt's. *Hers.*

Two of my great-grandmother's daughters were forbidden from getting married because their lives were to be sacrificed for her: one daughter was to work to provide financial support and the other was required to stay home and nurse her. Spinsters, destined to a life of caregiving and loneliness, doing what my Teta's father had failed to do. Teta spared my mother that fate.

My Teta Nour had been pulled out of school in fourth grade to learn how to become a seamstress. She never learned to read or write properly, could barely sign her own name and did not have a birth certificate, so we never knew for certain how old she was—but she did learn how to sew beautifully. Teta would knock off many designer dresses for me when I was young. I still remember being desperately in love with a white Chloé number from an expensive store. My mother and I bought it so Teta could sew a perfect replica, and then returned the original.

Victoria forbade Teta from putting on makeup or wearing heels. A young woman innocently socializing with the opposite sex was the same as a young woman choosing a life of prostitution. There are no shades for Middle Eastern women: you are either all or nothing, good or bad. Even laughing too much was a display of unbridled frivolity that could land a girl in the bad category. At her core, my grandmother rebelled against this dichotomy. Teta would leave the house, put makeup and heels on, go about her day, and change back before returning home. She was precocious and a little flirtatious and desperate for a bit of adventure. Maybe that is why Victoria finally allowed her to go on a trip with the local

church. For some reason or other, that trip fell through, and Teta was heartbroken. As consolation, Victoria sent Teta, with her older brother as chaperone, to visit cousins in the big city of Cairo. Young women in much of the Middle East never go anywhere without being chaperoned by a close male relative. It was there that Teta first laid eyes on my motorcycle-riding, leather-jacket-wearing grandfather, Mounir, who followed her around the entire time. Smitten, he wanted Teta to stay in Cairo, but she knew it was forbidden. When she returned to Jerusalem, my grandfather quickly followed, begging Victoria to let him marry Nour. Teta Vicky wouldn't permit it. So my grandfather went home and persuaded his mother to travel with him to Jerusalem and to plead on his behalf for my grand-mother's hand in marriage. She did, and Teta Vicky relented, but not before warning her daughter that without any family around her, she was sure to be killed in Cairo. Teta went anyway. She was eighteen years old.

Initially, my grandmother took to the bustling streets of Cairo, but soon became homesick for her family and her mother. In her ninth month of pregnancy with my mother, she and Gedo had packed everything and were about to move to Jerusalem to be with Teta's family. But on the eve of the move, my mother insisted on being born in Cairo. She wasn't going to give up on urban living that easily. Teta and Gedo did move to Jerusalem, though, where two sons were born, but after four years in the city, Teta knew it was not for her or her family anymore. So she and my grandfather uprooted themselves and three children again and moved back to downtown Cairo.

This time Cairo took, and Teta eventually even moved two of her sisters there, while the rest of her siblings moved to Jordan. It was there that she had a fourth child, my uncle Sami, a distant and accidental afterthought.

My grandmother's life in Egypt was good. Gedo, a mechanic by trade, grew a successful trucking business that provided my grandmother with a very comfortable lifestyle. But if being a mechanic was my grandfather's trade, being a womanizer was his hobby, and an entirely acceptable one by Egyptian male standards. He was good-looking and cool and flirtatious. My young Teta, beautiful and tough as nails, would have none of it. Early on, it was clear who was the head of that household, and it wasn't Gedo.

Despite her simple upbringing, Teta grew into her life in Egypt. She was always beautifully dressed, kept her home in perfect order and frequently redecorated. The children all had tutors that my Teta hired in the hopes that at least one of them would be academically inclined. None of them especially were, but they did well enough, with the two middle sons becoming general accountants. My mother, the only daughter, was sent to a French school in Cairo, and she grew up spoiled and well taken care of. Her summers were spent on the beach in Alexandria, her weekends at the souk buying fabric for her next dress. But it was the proverbial gilded cage. The only dream she was allowed to have was to find a husband after high school. Throughout it all, Teta ruled the family with an iron fist. She was the single strongest influence in my mother's life and Uncle Sami's life and a powerful one in mine. She restricted my mother, didn't understand Sami but loved him unconditionally, and me, for some reason, she encouraged to be free, to travel, to be adventurous, and not to settle down and get married.

"*Ya Hayati,*" Teta would say whenever she saw me, her first grandchild. "My Life." Unlike the antiseptic "darlings" and "dears" of the English language, endearments in Arabic are raw. More than a name, they are an expression of how much you mean to someone, how cherished you are. I cringe when someone flippantly calls me "dear" as though it were nothing more than a dog whistle. *Ya Hayati. Ya Amar. Ya Rohi.* My Life. My Moon. My Soul. This is how we speak to each other in my culture. This is how my Teta spoke to me.

Teta and I spent most of my early years being virtually inseparable. I was in her apartment on Thorncliffe Park Drive every single day as she took care of me while my mother and father were at work. She had started taking English lessons and would take me with her, depositing me in the playroom.

It had one of those half doors, and I would crawl under it, desperately looking for her, the thought of our separation for even an hour was unbearable. When I started school, I spoke a mash-up of Palestinian and Egyptian dialects, but not a word of English. I spent the whole first day crying in class, unable to understand what anyone was saying, while Teta spent the whole day crying outside the classroom until we could be reunited at the end of the school day. My early report cards describe a shy and quiet girl. Who did they meet back then? Whoever that was, she is long gone, I think.

The life Teta had enjoyed in Egypt could not be replicated in Canada. Most of the money supporting that former life had dissipated—and the transatlantic back-and-forthing had pretty much sapped their savings. When they arrived permanently in Canada, my grandfather had to return to being a mechanic, and the elegant lifestyle my grandmother had enjoyed disappeared forever. In suburban Toronto, Teta was back to cooking and cleaning and sewing as she had done in Jerusalem.

Initially, we lived in the same apartment building as my grandparents, a few floors down. Dad commuted to work for a while from Toronto to London, Ontario, until he got a position in Brantford at a large pharmacy chain in a department store. My parents moved there briefly, but both my mother and Teta found the distance unbearable, and after that brief separation, I never lived far from Teta. That was how it was until well into my teenage years.

The first house that my parents bought was a brown semi-detached on Mallaby Road in North York, a suburb just north of Toronto. My parents were very proud that they had bought the last house in the new subdivision. "It is the best one," they would say, "because it is the 'model' home." Who could blame them? It came complete with lime green and orange shag rugs after all. Walking into the house would land you in a small square of a foyer covered floor to ceiling in mirrored tiles with gold veining. Up three stairs and you could walk into the kitchen or, dangerously, into the living room, an unthinkable transgression unless we had guests. "Living room" is a misnomer. It was neither occupied by the living nor lived in. Take another five steps up and you were in the bedrooms, which were separated by the smallest of hallways.

We had not one but two basements, one at street level and one below ground. Basements are important to us ethnics. It is often where the second, real kitchen is kept. For Arabs, it was where children should be kept. The first basement was done in dark wood panelling, a suburban staple. This was where I spent most of my summers and any spare time I had. For me, summer camp was the basement. But a few stairs below, the second basement . . . that was a whole other thing. I had persuaded my parents to try something new and install light wood panelling down there. Maple was more *Amerikani*, I argued. And in an epic break with tradition, they did. Uncle Sami, always more than a little extra in everything he did, convinced my parents that rotating multicoloured disco lights were also an absolute must. A hidden disco in suburbia! And there the second basement sat, with disco lights and maple panels ready to go, largely unused the entire time we lived on Mallaby Road. Except by me. I spent a lot of time in that basement practising my dance moves all alone, except when Teta would occasionally join me.

Teta and Gedo moved to a semi-detached three-bedroom house almost identical to ours, just down the street. In it, my grandmother's life was one of repetition. Clean. Cook. Clean up again. She hated the routine of it, how stifling and boring it was, but it was expected of her and it was all that was left for her here. She would wash every countertop, vacuum every shag carpet every day until it was spotless, and when she came to our house, she would look on disapprovingly, noting that my mom—who my friends always said was a neat freak—was too slow to clean up and when she did, not thorough enough.

When my parents decided to move to a detached house a whole street away, Teta was not happy. But our new house backed onto a ravine, and on the other side of the ravine was my grandmother's house. I could literally wave to her from the balcony. It still felt too far, though—for her and for me. Most days after school I would go to her house. Most weekends I would sleep over. When my grandfather was injured in two accidents (a car he was working on fell on him, and later he slipped off a ladder and broke his neck) and had to stay in the hospital, I was sent to stay with Teta, who was too frightened to sleep alone. I don't know what protection I could ever have provided, but then again, since a young age, I'd always been sent to accompany my father when the alarm at his pharmacy went off in the middle of the night. We would wait together for the police to arrive. I think my family has always thought I could do much more than I really could. Somewhere along the line, I must have come to believe it.

I loved having Teta to myself. She woke up every day at six and started baking. God help you if you thought you were going to sleep in; she viewed sleeping in as a sign of laziness, especially in children. And so I was up at dawn sitting in the kitchen with her while she made pita and labneh (a Middle Eastern type of cream cheese), *lahmajeen* or my favourite, *'aish* with za'atar. It's funny to see labneh and za'atar on so many restaurant menus these days. I was embarrassed about my foreign lunches in elementary school and would do my best to hide them. I complained enough about our Arabic lunches that my mom eventually relented, and from that point on my brother, six years my junior, and I were sent to school with two pieces of toasted bread, a Kraft cheese slice in between (occasionally with butter if Mom was in a good mood), and two chocolate chip cookies wrapped in tin foil. Two *stale* chocolate chip cookies. "Chip" is always pronounced *ship* in true Arabic fashion—replacing *ch* with *sh* is for me a sure giveaway that someone is Middle Eastern. Mom and I would routinely rehearse: "Ship as in two ships passing in the night, chip as in potato chip." Try as I might, to this day she says *sh*ocolate *ship* cookies. If Pete or I ever complained, this little bit of luxury was forfeited for a few days as punishment for our lack of gratitude. When we reminisce these days about our miserable school lunches, my mother is unmoved. "You didn't starve," she says. My love of cooking—the primal satisfaction that comes from feeding my family—came from Teta, not my mother.

A great deal of my time was spent with Teta engaging in her favourite pastime: shopping. I come by it honestly. Shopping anywhere for anything still consumes me. In those days, we would go to the St. Lawrence or Kensington food markets. Long before either of these places were trendy, this was where we immigrants shopped. Ethnic food shopping is a weeklong activity, involving going to numerous shops in search of the best prices. So it was downtown to Kensington and St. Lawrence for fish and meat, and up north to Knob Hill Farms (pronounced *Knobba* Hills Farms by my Teta, who added an *a* to the end of most words) for fruits and vegetables.

But the best time, when Teta was in her zone, was when we went to a flea market (*flea'ah* market). It was there that Teta's negotiation skills were in full flight, skills that surpassed those of any lawyer who has spent a thousand hours studying mediation and negotiation. This was where she excelled. For Teta, the art of bargaining, for anything, was a sign of your mettle, your intestinal fortitude.

I inherited my love of negotiation from Teta. My grandmother was so skilled at the art of negotiation that she was able to return a carpet that she had used for eight years to the department store because she didn't like the colour anymore. With her fierce mix of Arabic and English, she always got what she wanted. As for paying full price for any item of clothing, that was just unthinkable—only *Amerikani* did that. Sometimes she negotiated, and sometimes the price tag would magically fall off an item and Teta would ask how much it was. When the cashier would give her the price, Teta would say that it had been on the sale rack. Blatant price switching was routine for her because, really, why should Hudson's Bay charge more than what Teta thought something was worth? She always won. It wouldn't be until years later that I would come to understand price switching is a crime (I've defended people charged with this offence). But in Teta's hands, it was an art form. It was as though she were back in the Cairo souk. I have of course atoned for my accomplice role in this bit of petty larceny by paying obscene amounts of money for clothing all at full price.

This was usually how I spent my days with Teta but every summer, like clockwork, a malaise would set in. Teta missed the beach visits to Alexandria, the neighbours coming by unannounced, the chicken at Andrea, an outdoor restaurant on the outskirts of the pyramids where the cooks, sitting cross-legged around a fire on the dirt floor, would magically turn balls of dough into puffy, steaming pita. She missed home terribly. She remembered how much she had given up. This yearly proclamation of boredom invariably heralded our attempt to distract her with a pilgrimage to Niagara Falls. It was all the creativity my family could muster.

As with all family events of my youth, attendance was not optional. When the call came, my extended family all reported for duty. For us, Niagara Falls was an adventure to a foreign land. We might as well have been packing up and driving out to Alaska. Preparations would have begun a few days before: who had the coolers, who was driving, what time we were leaving, who was bringing the barbecue. The logistical complexities were many, but eventually coolers full of Middle Eastern mezze, pita, chicken, and shish kabobs showed up along with a small round barbecue that would be precariously pitched on a tripod. Yes, we could have just bought food in Niagara Falls, but that would be about as unimaginable as reaching into a minibar in a hotel or, God forbid, ordering room service. The five-car caravan—my parents, grandparents, and uncles' families—would assemble early in the morning at Teta's house. Although we always

planned to leave early, that never happened. By the time we cousins jockeyed our way into each other's cars, and the trunks were filled with the food, the adults were already exhausted and annoyed.

Niagara Falls was no small trip for us. But it was at least a manageable one, with a direct route on a single highway. Except not really. We'd be loaded into the back of my parents' Pontiac Parisienne, crammed together on the bench seats with one of us always ending up squished on an adult's lap in the front. No seat belts of course. Like clockwork, about forty-five minutes into the drive, one of the cars would have the audacity to break the caravan line causing the adults to stop yelling at us long enough to notice. This would cause another car to pull over to the side of the road and the others to follow suit. And by the side of the road, an argument would invariably break out, discussions about what to do—*Where did they go? They were just here! Why do they always do this?* And after arriving at no solution, but allowing my dad enough time to have a smoke, everyone would pile back into the cars and continue on . . . only to find the occupants of the errant car sitting at our usual picnic spot. And when we were reunited, well, it was as though we had been apart for years. *Ah lan weh sahlan, ya halweh.* Losing a member of the family, even for an hour, was unthinkable. By the time we arrived, everyone was miserable—except Teta, who had satisfied her need for adventure, to go out of the house, to go anywhere.

If you are thinking that the attraction of Niagara Falls was the natural wonder of the falls themselves, you would be wrong. The main selling feature for us was accessibility. It was a straight line on the highway from our house to there and, frankly, it was all the Canadian adventure we were able to muster. Cottage country was as exotic as France. One year, my parents decided to venture out to cottage country to visit one of my mother's brothers. My parents got lost on the highway, got into an argument, and drove straight back home. They never ventured to the distant land of cottage country again. And the truth is that it took twenty years and multiple arguments for my parents not to lose their way getting to the airport. My father remains befuddled that a road called Airport Road does not actually lead to the airport at all. He finds this a linguistic abomination. "The Unilinguals," he mutters every time.

These small trips did little to soothe Teta's chronic restlessness driven in part by the reality that she couldn't quite acclimatize to her new surroundings in this country. The lack of community, the desire for everyone to live on their own and have space and privacy—that was confusing to her. I grew up in a house where shutting a bedroom door was viewed as an odd North American behaviour seen as exclusion, not privacy. I still have an aversion to shutting doors. We lived *together* and the idea of alone time was completely foreign. Teta in particular was surprised by the North American custom of calling before visiting someone or making a specific appointment to socialize. In Egypt, no formal invitations were ever extended and family and visitors always appeared at your door and around the dinner table. Multi-generational and extended families were part of life. Not here. Teta was on her own. My uncles were building their own lives, moving away, and only my mother remained close with her.

In the early 1980s, my mother did not want to work in a bank anymore and Teta was equally tired of the monotony of cooking and cleaning all day. And by then, we had seen people on TV living the North American dream. For the young ones, education was the way in, but the older generation believed that starting a business would bring success. My family had no business experience or understanding of retail, but there was one thing that my mother and Teta knew well. In fact, they had been in training for this their entire lives. We were expert shoppers. And so my uncles, grandparents, and mom got together and opened our one and only family business: La Chatelaine Fashions, a woman's clothing store. I'm sure you've heard of it. Not.

The store was located in a strip mall where true fashion goes to die. The one upside of the location, however, was that the competition was slim to none. Up the street was Bargain Harold's, a place that sold overstock and knock-off brand name clothing dumped into huge bins for shoppers to sort through. I know this because back then much of my wardrobe was from there. My family was convinced that we could corner the fashion market in our small sliver of suburbia, one sparkly gown at a time. And my mother and Teta had glitter bred in the bone from the days of wandering the souk in Egypt.

Teta now had a legitimate reason to shop and, more importantly, get out of the house. She would travel to New York and spend days shopping in the garment district and bring back beaded evening gowns and purses galore. Once back in Toronto, she would work the floor of the store with my mother, selling dresses and doing the necessary alterations in the evenings. I, of course, spent a lot of time working in the store with Teta, inseparable as always. La Chatelaine really was my summer camp, immigrant style. While the strip mall did not have canoes and lakes, it had Teta, a bowling alley, and an art store. That was enough for me. I alternated my summer days between all three; working in the store with Teta to make a sale, bowling—which I wasn't half-bad at—and taking art classes where I learned decoupage and how to paint a two-foot high plaster collie. My mother always displayed my summer art projects prominently in our hallway until the collie had his nose broken and the decoupage art migrated to the basement never to be seen again.

For a while, the store did well enough that we opened a second store not far away. But eventually, it became clear that we couldn't compete with larger stores that had way more variety. And the demand for sparkly gowns in suburbia just wasn't burgeoning. So eventually, one store closed and then the other. And that was the end of my family's fashion empire, with Teta once again relegated to the kitchen—spending her days cooking and cleaning.

With this venture and others, we were just trying to get a fix on life here—how to be part of it, how to become North

American. We didn't know about the fancy neighbourhoods, the private schools, the establishment that runs so many things and whose habits and history were still largely foreign to us. And we had no awareness that anyone saw anything all that different about us, as though our accents, our skin colour, and what we ate were invisible. Teta kept us close at hand, grounded to a home that we all knew, to things that we understood. But even she couldn't prevent other things from pulling us into this country. We started to drift apart—our weekend dinners became less frequent, cousins moved away, and even those summer caravans to Niagara Falls eventually stopped.

As time passed, Teta and Gedo eventually could not keep up their house and moved to a condominium even farther north of the city. It was a nice apartment but completely soulless and isolated, even more so because Teta could no longer drive. She had tried and failed her driving test three or four times; on one occasion she actually drove through a garage door. Reverse and gas were too complicated. Then one day she came home and announced she had passed her exam. I'm convinced that she never took it and sent her sister, a doppelgänger, to take it instead. We never let her drive. And so there she was, deposited on the outskirts of the suburbs in a sterile condominium waiting for someone to come and visit. My mother did daily, and I did weekly.

Teta was in her early seventies when Mom began to notice that she was becoming forgetful. We explained it away for a while, put it down to old age, and then could no longer deny it. Alzheimer's was taking its grip. Teta was slowly disappearing— her personality, her mischievous wit—and someone else we didn't know was replacing her. When it became impossible for her to manage anymore, the decision was made to find her a home. This is painful in any culture; in ours, it is unthinkable. The care of its elderly is one of the places North American culture collapses as the pandemic demonstrated. In many countries, because of custom and economics, aging parents—their well-being, care, entertainment, health—become the responsibility of their children. It is payback time. The elderly are respected and protected, and it is the duty of children to assume that responsibility.

The pain of placing my Teta in a home was unbearable for my mother. But it was as unavoidable as it was devastating. She was sent to a place called Cummer Lodge, and there she declined daily, losing her mind. I kept looking for it, as though if I looked hard enough I'd find it, there on a shelf, in a lost-and-found where all the lost minds are just waiting to be reclaimed, as though losing your mind were no more than an act of carelessness. I wanted to find her. I watched the slow, awful, humiliating erosion of her brain, her memories, her personality, her humanity. There were moments of memories from childhood, confusion, distress, agonizing moments of fear. All we could do was try to soothe her—and ourselves. And even in the throes of this slow decline, Teta would fight to emerge. Just a little bit of her. As though she were saying, *I am still here.* Insisting on getting her hair dyed and applying her expensive Lancôme cream. *I am still here.* Even in the final stages of the treachery of that disease, when she had lost every memory, when I thought I could not find her anymore, I would walk in and she would take my hand, kiss me and say "*Marmoura, Ya Hayati,* I missed you." *Marmoura* was her pet name for me. She forgot a lot, but she never forgot me. No one calls me *Marmoura* or *Ya Hayati* anymore. That was hers.

Mom would suffer through each and every visit with guilt. Guilt about putting Teta in that place and guilt about hating every moment of visiting her there. To this day, my mother cannot speak about it without heartbreak and guilt. In my mother's mind, Teta's decline is linked somehow with the move from her homeland.

And then, one day, Teta slipped away completely. She died, and not peacefully. I wrote the eulogy for her funeral but could not get through it so my brother delivered it. And with Teta gone, gone too were all those years that we were not from *there* and not quite from *here*. The in-between years. The years when I looked to Teta to anchor me in some way, to remind me of why I did not quite fit *here* but belonged *there*.

In the years after she was gone, one Arabic word after another slipped away. There are days when I see someone with their grandmother, the way they talk to her, the way they hang on to her, and I am envious. And I think maybe if I turn the corner really slowly in a Middle Eastern grocery store, I will catch a glimpse of her. I go to the Arabic grocery store sometimes just for that reason—to see my people holding on to their Tetas. It's stupid, I know, but I can't find it anywhere else. And sometimes I take my two Anglo boys (you would have to look hard to find the fifty percent Arab in them) and we walk through the store. They know the food—the labneh, the pita, the *lahmajeen*—but there are days I am frustrated, angry that they don't really know any of this history. That they do not sense that these are their people too. That this part of me, of them, is all gone. "Do you remember Teta?" I ask my oldest. "Of course," he says. "Then tell me," I say, "tell me what you remember." And he does. It gives me comfort that I did not imagine her. That my son remembers something of her, my Teta.

I am invited to a conference where an Israeli mother and Palestinian mother, both of whom lost their sons to the unending war in that region, chose to join their pain and describe how that pain is the same for any mother. As I listen, I am crying. I think at first it is because of their suffering. But then I am ashamed, because it is not. It is because, as the Palestinian mother is speaking, I realize I am not listening to the English interpreter—I am hearing my Teta. She is speaking to me. "*Can Ya Hayati*"—he was my life—the Palestinian mother says of her son. *Ya Hayati. Ya Amar. Ya Rohi.* But I can't quite catch all the words. I strain to, I can't. Except those. They don't fade away. Now I am listening to the interpreter *and* the Palestinian mother and I know I am losing my words—my Teta's language, my Teta. I strain harder. But I cannot catch it all. And at that moment, I know.

Without her, I am not from *there* anymore.

4

IT'S ALL ABOUT THE GLITTER

WHEN THE DOCTOR TOLD my grandmother Nour that it
was too dangerous for her to terminate an unwanted pregnancy, she was devastated. She went home, put on a black dress
and went into mourning for the next nine months, a sign of
the shame that she, a woman in her thirties, was having a
child. In the Middle East, female sexuality is a tightly controlled commodity for fear that a mere trickle of freedom

might cause the whole dam to burst and drown the country in raging, unbridled female sexuality. Pregnancy at my grandmother's age was seen as an embarrassingly flagrant display that she was still a sexual being.

Nine months later, undeterred by his inhospitable start, my uncle Sami was born. Nour would take Sami for a walk up and down the bustling alleys of Cairo's Khan el-Khalili souk, but too embarrassed to publicly claim her son, she had my sixteen-year-old mother push the baby carriage, pretending Sami was hers. From an early age, you see, he belonged to my mother too. And then to me.

The first image I have of Sami is an old photograph taken in Cairo. His big saucer-like eyes staring straight ahead from one of those stiff professional shots we take of our children to hold on to them in tiny increments. He is four years old, dressed in white shorts and a formal white shirt, standing on stairs, one knee on the stair above, one pudgy little hand holding on to the railing, looking far too stylish and defiant for his age. It was an early sign that he would never be contained, that he would remain utterly incomprehensible to my Middle Eastern family for the rest of his life. In all of those early family photos I have, Sami is always standing to the side, not in an isolated, sad way but as if to say, *Look at me*.

Sami was removed in every way from his older three siblings—in style, temperament, and age. My mother was the oldest, followed closely by her two brothers, and then there was a lengthy gap until Sami was born. My mother was then in her mid-teens, and my two uncles were already young men and well on to their own grown-up lives. They are both accountants—conservative, traditional men who were happy to come to Canada, anglicize their names, and try to blend in.

Sami, on the other hand, saw the move to another country as a chance to finally get noticed. The furthest thing from a fiscally responsible accountant, Sami never met a dollar that he couldn't spend. He didn't look like his siblings either. He more closely resembled me and my brother—dark, clearly foreign, not an angular WASPy feature to save his life—although he later tried with a nose job that successfully obscured his precise origin but did nothing to erase his ethnicity. He bore an uncanny resemblance to the designer Isaac Mizrahi.

Sami's history in Cairo was opaque to me, a jigsaw puzzle with too many pieces missing. I saw the general outline but never the full picture. He never reminisced about it fondly (or unfondly, for that matter) like the rest of my family, and I find myself to this day still trying to piece together his past as much as my own. Whatever friendships he had in Cairo were either fleeting or didn't leave much of an impression. I used to think that was because the steaming cauldron of the streets of Cairo is just not a place you let your children go out to play. But my uncles and my mother talk about their many friends. Where were Sami's? Did he not have friends, or was he bullied, or did he just not care to talk about it one way or the other? No one seems to know. And while my mother and her two other brothers cheerily reminisce about their summer trips to the beaches of Alexandria and how grand their life was in Cairo, it's as if they lived that life without him. Where was he? Why can't I find him there, in Cairo?

My mother offers something of Sami's early years, hinting that he was more drawn to the women in his life than the men. Sami spent much of his childhood with her and Teta wandering the souk shopping, helping my mother look for just the right beads or fabric for her next dress or a dye to match her shoes perfectly to her newest outfit. "Too much shopping for a boy," she says to me now, a hint of guilt in her voice. She blames herself. "There should have been more men in his life . . ." But then she stops herself short.

So the story of Sami for me begins when I came along. When I was born, Sami was all of ten years old. As the two youngest in the family, we became inseparable, like siblings. The family's move to Canada must have been a relief to him. There was just nothing inherently Middle Eastern about him except his looks. He did everything he could to lose his Arabic accent and become *Amerikani*. He embraced North America in a way the others in his family resisted. Alone among us, he did not ever have one foot in Egypt. He was thrilled to plant both feet firmly on North American soil. I do not think he would have survived in Egypt, although he would have surely figured out a way to escape.

Maybe that was part of the reason he had such a close connection with my mother. I don't think either of them could have thrived in Cairo. Outsiders, both of them. My mother was married and had given up any hope of an independent life by the time she came to Canada. Sami, on the other hand, was fourteen, and Toronto was as good a place to start as any. While the rest of the family was trying to acclimatize to this new world, Sami wasted no time shaking off the old one.

In my parents' first apartment, in Thorncliffe Park, I was almost always with Teta or Sami or both. Bored, Sami and I would spend countless hours playing dress-up. He would do my makeup and dress me in my mother's clothes that, on my child-sized body, looked like gowns. He would top it off by adding one of her wigs, magically transforming me into the shortest drag queen you've ever seen. He was a budding stylist/makeup artist, and I loved being his model. If Instagram had been around then, Sami would have been a star with a million followers. But all we had was a Polaroid camera to document his makeovers. There are pictures of me standing on our apartment veranda in full regalia—gloves, wig, dress. I could have sat there with him for hours being done and redone. A makeup chair is still one of the most comforting places on earth for me to be.

Reinventing and redoing places, people, and himself was at Sami's core. Nothing was sacrosanct, and nothing and nobody was beyond a makeover. It was Sami who insisted on redecorating our suburban house on Saddletree Drive. It was a soulless new build with lots of beige. My parents decorated it with the requisite dark wood panelling and furniture that we kids were not permitted to touch. We lived largely in the family room, the kitchen, and the TV room. Beige was the cruellest of colours for Sami—not so much a colour as an insult, a sign that one had given up on life. My parents acquiesced to having the whole house repainted white with the faintest pink undertones so that when the sun shone in, Sami would say, the house would be blanketed in a warm and life-affirming flush of pink. My brother Peter's bedroom curtains were torn down and replaced with silver blinds. My bedroom was given matching wallpaper and fabric with birds and flowers that, according to Sami, mimicked Marie Antoinette's bedroom. Why? Because that is what every suburban Arab girl needs and wants. Years later, when I visited Versailles, I was struck by how close Sami had come to the original. If he could have added a hall of mirrors, he would have—and he came close when he insisted on mirroring the tiny hallway entrance of our house. It was never going to be Versailles, but for just one split second when you walked in, maybe you could forget you were in suburbia.

Sami never did well at school, and my mother would later be convinced he had some undiagnosed learning disability. Shortly after or during high school, he decided he wanted to be an actor. This was the first of what would turn out to be many professional incarnations, all in some artistic field or other. In my culture, saying you want to be an actor is as good as saying you want to be unemployed for a living. There is a great deal of familial shame associated with the profession, exacerbated, no doubt, when your two brothers are accountants. My father's brother was a musician and his aunt was quite a famous comedienne in Egypt, but my mother refers to them as though they were freaks of nature, hiccups in the family line.

As testament to my grandmother's unconditional love for Sami, though, she stood by him, if not his choice of profession, and supported him as enthusiastically as she could. She went to his plays, although I am certain she didn't understand a single word. I, of course, insisted on tagging along, totally enthralled by him. I remember being in absolute awe as I watched Sami on stage the very first time. I think I was about eight or nine. He was good at it, and he loved the attention that came with being centre stage. In the very last scene of one of his plays, his character was stabbed. I was terrified he was hurt. At the end of the play, he took me around and introduced me to all the actors, and I still remember the retractable plastic knife he insisted on showing me to calm me down. I was convinced that one day he would be a star. He had a book called *The Great Movie Stars*. Inside, there is an inscription:

> Christmas 1972
> To Sammi—
> One day your photo and name will be in a book like
> this. All the best of luck to reach that star and become
> "A Clown".
>> Love
>> Martha Gleeson

I have no idea what the clown reference was all about or who Martha Gleeson was, but she misspelled his name. It was a bad omen when you're trying to make your way into a book organized alphabetically. When Sami gave up his dream of becoming an actor, he gave me the book. He had a habit of disposing of things and careers like that. I remember sitting on my bed and endlessly poring through the book's alphabetical pages. All the famous stars that my parents used to tell me about were there. But to me, the most important was Julie Harris, because I knew that one day, right before her name would be his—Sami Haddad.

During his acting phase, Sami became friends with an older actress named Ursula. They spent time rehearsing their parts and discussing the plays they were in but mostly designing costumes that Sami would sew for both of them. His stage name was Robert Ansari; he chose a name that began with *A* in anticipation of securing top billing for a movie that someday he would star in. Sami was more interested in the costumes than he was in acting (or in Ursula, for that matter), which came as no surprise to me. The headshots I have of the two of them are spectacular in their Las Vegas kitsch, but the costumes were killer heavy on the rhinestones and beading. Sami was wildly bedazzling before it became a thing.

Sami would take me with him when he and Ursula worked on their dance routines and costumes. She lived downtown, in an old, somewhat grand Victorian house that you had to climb a steep set of stairs to get to. I've driven around the city trying to find that place but never could. Things disappear if you don't make a point of hanging on to them. I remember Ursula, though. She reminded me of an aging Anita Ekberg except with reddish hair. She was kind to me and she had a stunner of a blond-haired daughter who would play with me while Sami and Ursula were rehearsing. I was just happy to tag along. That was my life then—always tagging along with Sami.

The acting went nowhere. Same with the dancing, the singing, the interior designing, and virtually every other job he tried his hand at. Not because he wasn't talented—he had talent in spades when it came to any artistic endeavour—but because he always got bored and wanted to move on. There were no fine arts schools in those days to develop his talents, to give him a base and environment to work from at an early age. Maybe his professional restlessness was a result of not getting the right education, of being considered a failure because he didn't fit into the academic mould. Or maybe my mother's theory wasn't so far off and he did have something like ADHD. I'll never know.

What I did know was that he was a rock star—a person who could find the fun and joy in the most mundane things in a suburban life that I hated. With Sami there, the weekend dinner at my grandmother's house would become a dance club or a cooking class or a dress-up party. He was a vortex of energy that woke our sleepy family. It wasn't the particular things he did that were special; it was the manner and spirit in which he did them. What is clear to me now is that he was struggling with being who he wanted to be—with being out or gay or bisexual. He never tried to act in any other way, even going so far as to bring "friends" home to stay. If the rhinestones and glitter and leather pants and insatiable penchant for animal print didn't give you a clue, then nothing was going to. You had to be wilfully blind not to see who he was.

But our effusive and oversharing Middle Eastern family could not bear to share that one thing with him. It was simply never discussed. I would only hear bits and pieces of his struggles later. Even with my well-honed cross-examination skills, I haven't been able to get at the truth of it—the pain Sami must have felt, how his lifestyle ran up against that of the rest of the family and nice suburban immigrants and Middle Eastern morals. I've been told how my father was sent to find Sami in gay bars and bring him home, and this story is told as an act of compassion, even heroism, on my father's part. A good and selfless deed. Dragging the prodigal son away from sin. I don't think my family understands who the real hero of that story is.

In 1970s Toronto, the gay scene was solidly underground. It was buried deep in the social fabric virtually everywhere except New York and San Francisco. Sami had no choice but to leave. I wonder whether, had he been given some breathing room, some support, he would have felt the need to escape at such an early age. But I realize not a single thing could have held Sami in Toronto. The city—buttoned up, conservative, homogeneous—was not right for him. He was bored and stifled and wanted to see what there was to see in the world. And so one day I came home from school and was told that Sami was moving to New York by himself. He had no job and no visa, just some money my grandmother had given him. He was eighteen.

I look at my sons now and cannot imagine what courage it took for Sami to come to that decision. Leaving his family, his home, with little money, no idea how he was going to survive. But that was the thing about him—for all his effeminate over-the-top fabulousness, he was one of the strongest and toughest people I have ever met. He was unafraid. Fearless. In North American culture, as in many, femininity, whether in a male or a female, is a sign of weakness. How wrong that is. It is much easier to be who you are when you have the comfort of being safely enveloped by the majority. Those who reveal themselves on the fringes, whether sexual, social, political, or artistic, they are the ones who demonstrate real bravery. Sami would always tell me that the toughest people he ever met were drag queens: glitter and shine on the outside but tough as nails through and through.

There is a decade's worth of gaps for me in this period of Sami's life, after he left us in Toronto and started over in New

York. I'm guessing he didn't want any of us to fill in those gaps, much like the gaps he left in Cairo. Other than when I went to visit him once a year or when he came home for Christmas or a surprise visit, his life in New York was a mystery to me—and even to Teta, who kept in constant touch with him. The things he did not tell me or anyone in the family about, I've tried over the years to piece together from photographs, piece-meal memories and bits of stories I can draw out of my family. I do know this: he was happy there. He fell in love with the city, the fashion, the endless availability of everything you could imagine and, most importantly, the freedom. His was a love story with New York.

But the real love story here was the one between Teta and Sami. My Teta never left him, no matter what. She was the single most powerful influence on him, the anchor that he would always return to. He told me one day that there was nobody in the world he loved more and hated more than Teta. He understood that she was his greatest champion, and he hers. When she would go to New York, his friends were thrilled that "mama" was coming. She would cook Middle Eastern food for them, and Sami would take her every-where—not just to tourist sites and shopping but to night-clubs and parties. He loved and cared for her. He was the one who bought her a dishwasher because he couldn't bear to see her standing and doing the dishes by hand anymore. He would come home from New York with surprises for her. One year it was a diamond ring wrapped in a gorgeous scarf because Sami thought she needed bling and my grandfather was never going to take care of my grandmother like that. He was the one who went with my grandmother on her one and only trip to Europe because he thought she needed to see Paris. Another year it was a puppy because he thought she was lonely. He never left her. Nor she him.

Shortly after Sami moved to New York, I learned that he had become friends with a woman and they had married so he could obtain a green card, a necessary move if he was going to make a life in New York. That was the first of his two marriages, his second to someone I believe that he loved. What the terms of that marriage were, I do not know. I do know that women always loved him.

With Sami's permanent move to New York City, my incessant whining to move there began. It would remain unabated for the next forty years. "Where do you want to go for a holiday?" my mother would ask. It was a silly question. I wanted to see Sami every chance I could get. And so starting at the age of ten, first with my family and then alone, I took almost yearly treks to visit Sami, first in his tiny basement apartment just past the Brooklyn Bridge and then to the East Side of Manhattan, near Bloomingdale's.

One year, Teta and I went to visit. Teta had heard that Sami had decided to become a vegetarian and she worried that this meant he had shaved his head and had joined the Hare Krishna. She was relieved that the only surprise we got when we arrived was the limousine Sami picked us up in. I had never been in one, of course, and Sami being Sami thought it was a necessary life experience. And outrageous that my parents failed me this way. Sami took me exploring on our own: under the Brooklyn Bridge, to a small Italian restaurant where he insisted I eat the most incredible manicotti that had ever been made; across the bridge, to the East Village, to Trash and Vaudeville which sold punk clothing; over to Greenwich Village to grab a slice of real NYC pizza; then to Fifth Avenue

where Maud Frizon imported shoes from Paris; and a last stop at a French bakery to pick up ficelle, a delicate thin baguette, before heading back home. It was limitless, the things we would discover, the things he would show me.

On another trip, he took me to One Fifth, an art deco–style restaurant decorated with fixtures from the luxury liner *Caronia*. But Sami's real goal was for me to try something called a truffle. It was Sami who took me to my very first museum, the Metropolitan Museum of Art. The two of us would stop in front of painting after painting, inventing hilarious backstories about the characters on the canvas. He insisted on immediately plucking my eyebrows because they were insulting him, and bought me glittery shoes that had the words *Too much is not enough* on the soles. He was the one who took me to Tiffany's and patiently stood by while I asked a bewildered sales clerk whether they sold mood rings, rings that change colour to reflect your current mood. Sami's feigned disdain that Tiffany's hadn't caught on to this jewelry craze was only exceeded by my disappointment. He would buy me dozens to make up for it.

And there was the evening he surprised my mother and me with tickets for a Broadway show, my first, a musical, of course—*My Fair Lady*. We wandered through Times Square, then into the theatre to our fourth-row seats. It was 1976 and I was eleven years old. If there was any question that I would forever be enraptured by New York, that one night sealed the deal. I had never seen anything like it. As we came out of the theatre, the entire city was sparkling. At least that is how I remember it. I didn't see the seediness of Times Square, the porn theatres, the drug dealers—only the sparkle.

Sami was still trying to figure out what to do with his life. Being a bon vivant with a penchant for shopping was not a viable way to make a living. Teta would fund his attempts at gainful employment as much as she could. There was no doubt in anyone's mind that he had talent, but the minute something was no longer done just for the pure fun of it, he put the brakes on. He tried singing and at one point was even training with an opera teacher. He was quite good at it, but then predictably lost interest. Next was a disco recording career. I would go to studio sessions with him, convinced he was going to be a star, but he soon drifted from that as well. I still have his recording of Donna Summer's "Last Dance." Interior decorating came next. He would get hired for jobs here and there. Mrs. Rosenberg, his elderly next-door neighbour, was obsessed with him, and after he redid her apartment she lined him up with designing job after designing job. He was fabulous at it, but as more and more people demanded his services, he once again got bored and bailed on the whole enterprise. His most sustained career was designing jewellery. He started by selling it on the street near Columbus Circle. When I would go and visit him, either alone or with my friend Rita, we would help him peddle his jewellery in the street until the police came by and we would have to change locations. With the growth of interest in costume jewellery, Sami's designs came to the attention of buyers from large department stores, and his little business moved indoors to his new apartment, a tiny one-bedroom in Manhattan, on Forty-Eighth between Lexington and Third Avenue. Then, like clockwork, Sami's interest faded away.

Sami's new apartment in a building called the Buchanan was the size of a postage stamp, but he loved it. In New York, apartment buildings have names and personalities, like people. Every year, without fail, he redesigned it into something more fabulous than before. The Buchanan had two of the most iconic and sought-after features in any New York apartment—a good old-fashioned doorman and a beautiful internal courtyard. It seemed so magnificent to me back then, that courtyard. Many years later I went back there just to walk through it one more time. It took me two years of working myself up to take that walk. *One last time*, I told myself. The doorman let me through, and once more I wandered through that courtyard. Here is the thing, though: I didn't feel anything this time. It was still beautiful, but I didn't feel Sami there, and somehow the place had shrunk in the last thirty years. I wasn't looking for the courtyard, I was looking for him. I will stop doing that one day.

But there was once magic in New York City. I hadn't ever seen *that* in Toronto. In the late 1970s and early '80s, when night fell, the city was a true democracy; it was where celebrities, ordinary folk, glamorous women, beautiful gay boys, the weird and wild and wonderful and ordinary would come together and celebrate being. Everybody wanted to be a star in New York's club scene. This democratization of glamour and glitz was new and heady, decades before social media where anyone and everyone could make themselves accessible, be seen and become famous. Back then, this intermingling of the rich and famous and the regular was happening on the floors of nightclubs.

The entrance table in Sami's apartment was always littered with invitations to these places—Studio 54, the Limelight, the Palladium, Danceteria. As a teenager in suburban Toronto, my fantasy was to get to those clubs, Studio 54 being the mecca for all that was fabulous and sparkly. Oddly, it was none other than my Teta who ended up clubbing with Sami. She would come back from her visits to him, sit down at her Formica kitchen table, as far removed from excess as one could be, and tell my mother and me about what really went on behind those velvet ropes. One night, the theme at the Limelight was religious, and Teta told us she spent the night dancing with a lookalike Jesus. Another night it was Roman, and she danced with clubgoers dressed in togas. None of it shocked her. She loved the fun, the dancing, the vibrancy, the inherent strangeness of the whole scene. It still seems bizarre to picture Teta on the dance floor in those hedonistic clubs, as far removed from her conservative Palestinian upbringing as she could possibly get but maybe that was exactly where she dreamt of being when she escaped her mother, put on lipstick, and walked around Jerusalem. Sami had a way of freeing up those around him, of getting them—my grandmother, myself—to do things we would never have thought of doing.

I never got to Studio 54 or the Limelight, but there was one nightclub that Sami did take me to later. The Pyramid had opened in the East Village in 1979 and it was the red-hot centre of the drag scene in New York. This was long before *RuPaul's Drag Race* was wholesome family viewing. Much of what happened in late-'70s New York was not for family viewing. At the Pyramid, the full force of drag, cabaret, and camp coalesced. The door was usually manned by a glorious drag queen, and inside, in addition to the show, there would be the most incredibly dressed queens dancing on the bar. The goal was to be more glam, more outrageous, and more camp than the person next to you. I would prepare by shopping at vintage thrift stores and then spend the evening dressing up, Sami doing my makeup, and then off to the club with him, often accompanied by my friends Laura and Rita. It felt completely and utterly normal. I didn't think of it as alternative or daring at all. It was where Sami went, where I went and where I had some of the most fun of my life. No stress, no sexualization, no judgment. And then I would fly back home, put on my school uniform and head to my Catholic girls' school, already counting the days before I could go back to New York again.

The incongruity of it all: drag bars in New York City, a Catholic girls' school in suburban Toronto. We are not one easily identifiable thing. Sami was not. I certainly am not. I spent years attempting to reconcile these parts of myself— the side liberated by my visits to Sami, the serious student and then lawyer—and I've gotten nowhere trying. It is inexplicable to me. That's the thing about Sami. He didn't feel the need to rationalize or explain himself. He was what he was, and he couldn't be that in Toronto so he left for the possibilities offered by New York. That is what drew me to New York, that possibility. It still does. That is what tied Sami to me. It was his gift.

This was my life until I was twenty-one. After two years of university, I was accepted to law school. As a reward, my parents agreed to let me go to Europe for a couple of months with my friend Rita, just before we both started school. We spent our days walking and our nights clubbing, stumbling into our bed-and-breakfasts in the early hours of the morning. For the first time in our lives, we experienced the breathtaking freedom of wandering in and out at any time. For years, when I had come home after a late night, I would see the hall light on in our house and know that my mother would be perched like a hawk on the top stairs or, worse, sewing. If my mother was sewing at two in the morning, it was never a good thing. I hated it. There is no sneaking in or out of an Arab home. And yet now I subject my own boys to the same thing. I forgive my mother and tell my sons that this hawk-like perching is genetic.

After starting our trip in England, Rita and I backpacked our way through France, ending up in Nice. I am not particularly interested in mystical things, but I have an odd fixation with fortune-tellers. It's a game for me. I find the fault in most of what they predict and it confirms my long-held suspicion that there is nothing very spiritual out there anyway. So when I stumbled on one in Nice—there are many—I went in and sat down and was prepared to be dismissive as the woman began telling me about myself and my family. I have largely forgotten what she said except for one thing: she turned over the Death card and said, "Someone in your family is very ill." She refused to read the cards after that. I was sure nobody was ill and she was a fraud, but on the off chance that I had hit upon the one real psychic in the world, I called home. Mom answered and told me that Teta had gone to New York to bring Sami home. He had recently been hospitalized with pneumonia and was very sick.

This is where I'd desperately like to stop. I know that Sami would prefer if I jumped past this next part and told the rest differently, dripping with glitter and excess and a good dose of fantasy. But that is not how the story goes.

When I got home from Europe, my mother told me that Sami had HIV. No one knew much about it back then. This was the early days of AIDS, and in Toronto, as almost everywhere else in the world, the only thing we knew was that it was a fatal disease infecting gay men predominantly in New York and San Francisco. The media called it the gay cancer.

When Sami came back from New York he was frail and thin. It had been his second bout with pneumocystis pneumonia, and he had been hospitalized each time. My family didn't know where to start. Some were worried it was contagious. My grandfather was convinced that the disease could be beaten if only Sami would stop being lazy and get a job. (He's not big on modern medicine. He was later convinced that his wife's Alzheimer's was just her trying to annoy him.) Teta did what she did best—she cooked for him to fatten him up. And my mother, in her quiet, resolute way, quit her job so she could spend all of her time with him. Sami's brothers were supportive, from a distance, but didn't discuss it much and tried to pretend that he was just fine.

There were days, even months, when Sami appeared to be somewhat healthy. "He's getting better," Mom and I would say. "He'll be able to go back to New York soon." We never discussed his illness directly with Sami, just kept to vague inquiries about how he was feeling, encouragement that he was getting better. All useless, unhelpful, and profoundly delusional. It was all the understanding that we could manage. But Sami knew the truth and was aware of how the story, his story, would end. There was only one likely ending back then. He had been to his friends' funerals in New York. He had given up his apartment, and with it his life there and any hope of returning. He knew. Now he was stuck in the very place he had fled, suburban Toronto, living with his parents, in his old room.

I went to nearly every doctor's appointment with Sami. He had been assigned to a knowledgeable specialist at North York General Hospital who had a few HIV patients. In those early days, having the virus meant that you were classified depending on your white blood cell count: you either had AIDS-related complex or full-blown AIDS. When we first went to the doctor, Sami's white blood cell count was sufficient to qualify as AIDS-related complex, meaning there was hope that his body could keep fighting. But that hope quickly faded, and he was soon reclassified with full-blown AIDS, a death sentence. I was with him when his doctor told him there was nothing left to do.

He was in and out of the hospital throughout the next eighteen months. Enrolled in the only available trial for the new drug AZT meant he was getting either the drug itself or a placebo. At the time we didn't know that an underground group had developed where HIV patients would exchange pills just to make sure they got whatever new drugs were floating around, while others were trying the various cocktails on offer that in some miracle combination might work. Sami dutifully took his allotted pills and did not improve one bit. Unfortunately, dosages of AZT given in the trial were often so high that a number of participants died faster *because* of the drug. I've always believed that Sami was one of those.

Besides law school, I spent the summer working as a waitress, first at Swiss Chalet and then Pickle Barrel so that my flexible shifts would allow me to spend time in the hospital; by January of my first year of law school, Sami was in and out constantly, trying to get his condition somewhat stabilized. His presentation was pneumocystis—the recurring bouts of pneumonia characteristic of HIV. Others struggled with Kaposi's sarcoma, a skin cancer that covered the patient with lesions. But these were just the warm-up events. HIV comes with numerous debilitating secondary presentations. In Sami, you could see that the virus was winning. There is a look to a person who is losing the battle to AIDS. It's called wasting because the person literally begins to waste away, in front of your eyes. To this day, I recognize it in people because I stared at it for two years, a gauntness in the face, a frailty to the body that pains me beyond belief. It is different from the look of someone struggling with cancer or another terminal condition. I cannot explain it, but I know it, or think I do and it always breaks my heart.

Throughout the ravages of this awful disease, throughout the lack of compassion and understanding from the rest of society and from many in the medical community, throughout the complete social isolation, Sami would not stop being fabulous. He couldn't if he tried. He insisted on finding the joy in the mundane. He would dress for his medical appointments as though he were going out on the town, usually in a black beret with an oversized black scarf and leopard-print shoes with huge buckles. Even on the road to his own death, Sami was going to make a stunning entrance. We went to a drag club in Toronto to celebrate Halloween together. He insisted on redesigning my parents' house (again) because he could not bear the furniture. We shopped together, endlessly. He turned every dinner party and meal at my grandmother's into a dance party. He kept telling me to lighten up. He couldn't bear my boyfriend and was shocked, astounded, that he did not treat me properly. "How hard is it," he would say, "to buy a small gift and throw it under the Christmas tree?" He would sit me down and insist that my eyebrows needed urgent plucking, my hair needed dyeing, that we needed to try the newest hottest restaurant. Or shop for Cornish hens at midnight just because we could. All of this while pulling his ravaged body out of bed each day, exhausted and sick. Some days he could not, and I would go out and buy something, some French pastry, some magazines, anything, and spend the days in his bedroom studying on the floor until he felt well enough to stand again.

Sami could not keep the weight on, and no drug was working for him. Day by day, he dwindled away, his beautiful clothes getting looser, his thick curly black hair getting thinner. I want to tell you the things about AIDS that they don't tell you about. The things Sami would not want you to know; the things that we have so graciously been allowed to forget. They do not tell you that in the final throes of the disease, the virus, after eating what is left of your body, attacks your brain. Sami would have terrifying bouts of dementia that would come on all of a sudden and just as suddenly disappear and he would come back to me. They do not tell you about the shaming. But how could you miss it when everyday in the hospital, the clank of the food tray left on the floor outside his door said it all. They do not tell you that this burden will be borne largely alone, maybe secretly shared in some community hall where a few have gathered to try to understand what was happening. You will go there alone too, as Sami did. They do not tell you of the hopelessness, desperation when young man after young man is buried, and you are told it is a curse visited on you for your sins, that this punishment is deserved. And all this, Sami bore with resilience, strength, and, of course, grace. Maybe that is why when the hospital kindly sent Sami home with a video that gruesomely and graphically explained what was coming next, Sami watched it alone and refused to let any of us see it.

In the last stages of this horrid disease, after your body and mind are gone, HIV keeps picking away. What is left of you? What else to cannibalize? Near the end, Sami went blind. That was what was left in the hospital bed of my beautiful uncle. My grandmother could not bear it. His brothers did not understand it. And my mother could not watch it. I did. I sat in that hospital room. Then one day, they finally asked my mother and me if they could stop the nutrition that was barely keeping him alive. Teta agreed that it was time. He died four days later.

While he was on his deathbed, I helped plan his funeral. I thought he would have died all over again if he was subjected to an unfashionable mahogany casket and I couldn't trust anyone in the family to do it correctly. So I picked the casket and the flowers. At the funeral home, the director wanted to know what he was dying of. My family said cancer. It is what they still tell people and even themselves and their children. I said, "AIDS. He is dying of AIDS. His name is Sami and he is dying of AIDS." I feel a compulsion to scream it, even now.

The funeral was not fabulous. I wish it had been. I gave the eulogy. None of his friends from New York came because my family did not tell them. He died here with only us surrounding him. I remember he told me that so many of his friends asked that their ashes be surreptitiously scattered in

Bergdorfs or Saks. There's something deliciously subversive and joyful about that. I would have liked to do that for Sami. Give him the glittery end that he deserved.

I often wonder what Sami's life would be like now. How he could have been free right here in Toronto. How he would not have had to leave or escape us. The possibilities might have been endless. There are none for him now. He is not here to see me or any of my accomplishments. Of all the people in the world who would have had a blast with my small and unexpected bit of notoriety and fame, it would have been Sami. He would have loved every moment of it—although I am sure he would tell me that I'm far too understated and serious. He would have wanted me to be *extra*, as the Millennials say. He would have made sure of it.

For ten years after Sami died, I could not say his name. All the pictures of him were put away because I could not look. All of his things boxed up. When my first son was born, I decided that his middle name had to be Sami. I told my family it was to honour my uncle, but I will tell you the real reason. I wanted an excuse to say Sami's name out loud again. And I do. I know that he doesn't hear me, but I will keep saying it, every day, just the same.

5

THE LIQUOR CONTROL BOARD

EVERY STORY NEEDS A HEROINE, and my mother is the heroine of this one. Evelyn wasn't the mushy bake-you-cookies-and-read-a-bedtime story kind of mom. I didn't know moms like that when I was growing up, and if she had been that kind of mother, I would not have been who I am. She is my best friend, trusted confidante, toughest critic, and the one person who told me repeatedly that women were not only equal to men but stronger and more resolute. She truly believes that to her core. According to my mother, my job in life is to demonstrate this very fact. Not once did she tell me to be sweeter, more feminine, less aggressive, or to stand down in any way. It never occurred to me to do any of those things, I think, because it never occurred to my mother.

To understand my mother, you must understand Middle Eastern mothers. They are a breed apart, tough, uncompromising, domineering, demanding, fierce protectors of their children and always, above all, never wrong. I learned that early in life. The main characteristic of this species of *materfamilias* is unrelenting irritation with and at everyone. Maternal irritability is as basic as falafel in my culture. Arab mothers float through each day in a perpetual state of frustration, bobbing in a sea of annoying children. Their days are filled with raising offspring, taking care of the household and managing their husbands. Certainly my mother's were. And Teta's. And every single Arab mother I have ever known. This contained and constrained existence accounts for their chronic case of irritability.

Annoyance is not just directed at their own children. It is generously showered upon the children of the world. A child that is crying in a store, whining, throwing a tantrum or interrupting adults is fixed with a stern gaze of disapproval. My Teta's gaze could wither flowers. Dig one layer beneath and you uncover profound disdain for the parents who allowed such a public display from their children. Dig down one layer further and there, just waiting to be unleashed, is the real judgment that a Middle Eastern mother has of North Americans—the parents are soft, relenting, weak. They focus *too* much on their children. I know that my generation spends obscene amounts of time and money on self-help books, parenting coaches and therapists, and as a result has mostly raised children to think that their rightful place is smack dab in the middle of the universe. But if you grow up believing you are at the centre of the universe, there is no place else to go. You've made it from the moment you were born. In my family, children were sidelined both physically and emotionally, somewhere on the far outskirts of the solar system. I grew up knowing that my needs were secondary to those of the adults around me, and I have spent my entire life working to get front and centre. I blame my mom. Or thank her. Some days, I don't know which.

Growing up, mommy-time alternated between getting out of the way while the housework was being done and getting dragged around from grocery store to shopping mall. I never felt I was missing out on my mother's attention or love; she just didn't have the time to outwardly display it. Her parenting parameters for each and every day required her to feed us and get us to bed. Everything in between was just biding time between those daily obligations. My mother always said, "I never loved you and your brother more than when you were sleeping." I think she would have been happiest if, after being born, Pete and I promptly went to sleep and didn't wake up until we'd graduated from law school. Make no mistake, she had our backs and loved us to her core, but being cheerful through the process of launching us into the world just wasn't part of the deal.

As a result, not upsetting my mother occupied a lot of time for Pete and me. It was nearly impossible *not* to annoy her. Most of the time, I couldn't blame her—and still can't. This was the dynamic of mother and child that I grew up with. A cheerful North American mother was quite simply not normal to me. I had seen them on TV—June Cleaver, Marion Cunningham of *Happy Days*—but seeing one in real life was as rare as running into a rainbow unicorn. Eventually, I started to catch sight of one every now and then. Like wood nymphs, they would appear, throw some glitter in the air and magically disappear. Growing up, I occasionally thought I wanted one of those happy singsong moms for my very own.

My commitment to family is attributable to my mother. Family was the centre of everything for her. We socialized together, fought together and travelled together. The travelling, especially, is a perverse obsession of mine. My mother is a nervous traveller, and I've made it my mission to make sure that she nervously sees something of the world, whether she likes it or not. Every two years, I declare that it is time to schedule our family trip. Not once has my brother been enthusiastic about this prospect, but he gives in anyway because he cannot bear the fit he knows I will throw if he refuses. Or the lecture about the importance of families being physically together. My mom also knows better than to resist. The trips always end up the same. By day two, my brother and I are annoyed because we have been surrounded by four screaming kids and cannot sit down in a decent restaurant without creating a scene. We are not naturally child-friendly in my family, and Pete and I spend an unconscionable amount of time thinking up excuses to get away from our own. Yes, it did take us five hours to find a bottle of water in Rome. My husband and sister-in-law, both WASPs, are dismayed by the way my family argues and then continues on as though nothing ever happened. Also, they are secretly ashamed of our manners, especially at airports. Arabs don't "queue" for anything. You just hustle your way to the front of the line. And then laugh at the WASPs, except ours who routinely dress us down for this behaviour. My mother is annoyed with my brother and me, well, just because that's the way she is. My father is suitably distant, emerging occasionally from his daily afternoon Scotch to tell a dad joke. Usually, it is the same joke for the entire two weeks. Mom complains to me that Pete is too sensitive. Pete complains to Mom that I am too high-strung. Pete and I find something to complain about regarding my dad. My husband generally ignores the lot of us, and my sister-in-law naps a great deal, most likely to get away from us. But we do this trek, year in and year out. And my mother frequently fondly says that she has seen the world with me.

I was not raised on a diet of Cinderella or princess stories. My mother did not think I should be saved by anyone. "Never depend on a man", my mother would repeat over and over. Not because men are inherently unreliable but because for her, financial independence and freedom were one in the same. And for a woman, the most important liberator and equalizer. Independence was to be my only objective. And princes, she said, never crack up to what they're supposed to be. So when I decided to get married, it came as a bit of a surprise to my mom. For her, the marital enterprise had to bring some tangible benefit to my life, and not in the traditional sense. Evelyn wouldn't have dreamed of thinking I needed supporting or taking care of. I was to have a career and be financially independent. She never deviated from that mantra. My father often worked seven days a week. No golf breaks for him or drinks with his buddies at the pub. Work and then home. Work and then home. Mom had her job; Dad had his. That's just the way it was. But it left my mother largely on her own to deal with my brother and me. This division of labour, she would say, is what she had signed on for. But not a contract she wanted for me. Marriage had one purpose, and that was to shore up my genetic stock.

A real blue-eyed North American boy would satisfy my mother's long-held dream: if I could not manage to look North American, the least I could do was marry the right person to give my offspring a fighting chance in the world. Looking "light" was a goal unto itself for my mother. Many racialized people have this internal conflict. It is easy to think it is just a form of self-loathing, but it is not. After years of colonialism and various iterations of oppression, we figured out that all the oppressors had one feature in common. Can you blame my mother for wanting it for her children too? *The unbearable whiteness of being. The unbearable being of whiteness.*

Years into my career, I was invited to a Canadian-Arab event. It was a night well attended by numerous politicians. I found myself talking to one of them. He knew of me and after chatting a bit about what I had been doing, he asked me why I was at this event. What was my connection to this group? I'm here, with my parents. We are Arabs, I told him. He was visibly stunned and without thinking, responded enthusiastically, *What a great story that is. We should tell more stories like yours. That is why this country is so great.* Whoever the "we" was, it clearly did not include me. The thing is that I hadn't told him what my "story" was. He had written it all on his own. In that moment. Upon hearing that I was an Arab. I don't know whether he thought my parents had parked their camel and hopped on a boat to experience the great riches of North America, but surely that is close to what ran through his mind. The story he had written in that moment had nothing to do with me or my history. And that one comment, in what was meant to be a compliment, I guess, he had said it all. Put me in my place. No matter how much you fly, you will be weighted down where you belong. *Not from here.* I was seething. I wanted to tell him my father, who was with me, speaks six languages fluently. My mother is a strong woman. We have worked hard. Our story is this country's story. I said nothing.

Camel. Sand N*. Dark One. Hebe. Paki. When is your dad coming to sweep the floor? I got all of those insults, as did my brother. Most people can't quite place us other than not from *here*. We know. We don't forget. I will never blame my mother

for trying, in her own way, to fix the obvious problem—to ensure her children had "access." To make us fit in. To partake in the land of milk and honey, your skin must be the color of milk and honey.

Blue eyes were the big get. As far as Evelyn was concerned, you could be a three-armed, one-eyed gorgon, but if that one eye was blue, *bingo*, you were marriage material. My father has blue-green eyes. Two of them. That, my mom would repeatedly tell my brother and me, is one of the main reasons she married him. Not the number, just the colour. It's true. He does have two nice blue-green eyes.

As a result of this maternal indoctrination, in high school biology class I became obsessed with Mendel's theory of heredity and recessive genes. Cross a dominant round pea with the recessive wrinkly pea, Mendel expounded, and you get a round pea three times out of four. My odds were brutal. I only had a one-in-four chance of getting a blue-eyed wrinkly pea. I was a bad genetic bet. Again, I blame my mother. She has brown eyes, as does her entire family. There's not a recessive blue-eyed gene in her entire genetic tree. My father brought renewed hope with his blue-green eyes, so you can imagine my mother's heartbreak when both my brother and I emerged from the womb with brown eyes. And dark hair and dark skin to boot. The round pea won. She refuses to admit it is entirely her fault and blames my dad, although I'm not sure on what factual basis. Unwilling to admit defeat, my mother determined to remedy her children's genetic failings by instilling in us the virtues of marrying blue-eyed partners to improve our genetic pool. How else were we going to get into all the country clubs, not to mention evade travel bans? It was her way of levelling the playing field.

I found one. Driving home after a lovely first get-together with my family and my distinctly blue-eyed soon-to-be-husband's family, my mother was unusually quiet.

Finally, she said, in Arabic, "You didn't tell me they were *that* white."

"I did. I told you they were Canadian."

"No, they are *real* Canadians."

"What is a real Canadian?" I asked.

"The children," Mom whispered, "they were all over the dinner table. They let the kids"—and here her voice faltered a bit—"eat with the adults. With the *adults*. Who were *guests*."

And there it was, the surest case of racial profiling ever. No need for genetic testing. No need for Mendel's theory of heredity. You want to know whether you are going to get a brown-eyed round pea or a blue-eyed wrinkly pea? Evelyn's theory of heredity. All you need to ask is one simple question: *When you sit down for dinner with guests, where do the children eat?* The answer tells you everything you could ever want to know about someone's ancestry. *They sit at the table? Oh, there must be some British in your lineage. The children are allowed to talk with adults at social gatherings? You must come from Celtic stock. A separate kids' table? Italian, or Middle Eastern maybe, but Mediterranean for sure.*

A few years later, my mother disclosed that she was shocked that my husband's family had a disturbing tendency to pay a lot of attention to their kids. By this she meant talk to them. In my family, as in any self-respecting Middle Eastern family, children were always relegated to the basement during get-togethers. The adults were to be on one floor enjoying adult time, the kids on another doing kid things. There was and always has been a separate kids' table. I don't think my brother and I graduated from ours until we were well into our twenties. Some days my mom says Pete and I should still be sitting there.

My mother is firmly convinced that the failure to ignore children has been chiefly responsible for a generation of mealy-mouthed kids. When my mother says a person pays a lot of attention to their children, it is not meant as a compliment. Obedience training of children in my family was achieved not by a backhand—although one was occasionally delivered—but rather by guilt. My grandmother wielded it like a samurai sword, as did my mother. Except my mother had perfected it with a modern twist—the silent treatment. In her hands, silence was a potent weapon that took the guilt trip to another level. I could spend an hour trying to pretend my mom's silent treatment wasn't happening, talking loudly, flapping around the room right under her nose, acting giddy as she ignored me for days on end. My brother can still go to extraordinary lengths pretending that the silent treatment isn't happening. He does this by going into hiding, the coward. But this show of bravado is always short-lived. In the end, we break and apologize. Because no matter what, my mother is always right.

Growing up in Egypt, my mother was always a bit of an outsider. For one thing, she didn't fit the bill when it came to her looks. She also didn't possess the natural gregariousness of my father, but rather a reserved air to hide her unease with other people. The only goal my mother's family had for her was that she get married. There was no interest in allowing a young woman in Egypt to have a single person's life experience. She was, in that Middle Eastern way, never alone. If she went to a party, she would be accompanied by her two brothers. She was not allowed to go out on dates or have any sort of life independent of her family. She'd finish school and then get married. She'd move straight from her parents' home to her husband's home. That was how women were raised. Even today, with more women educated and working in Egypt, a woman who lives alone is an anomaly.

My parents did not have an arranged marriage, at least not in the classic sense. My mother's family did not go out and find a suitable groom whom she was required to marry. She was allowed some choice in a husband, but no choice when it came to getting married. She met suitor after suitor, considering after each brief meeting whether this was the person she wanted to spend the rest of her life with. These auditions also involved the potential suitor meeting my mother's parents. If he made it past the first cut, they would find out about his family and arrange to meet them. It was only after they became engaged that the couple would be allowed to go out to dinner or a movie together unaccompanied. My father met my mother's requirements—he was educated, very bright and funny, and turquoise-eyed. And my mother was a catch. At twenty-one, she was a good girl from a good family who would make a compliant wife. Or so my father thought.

Being compliant isn't in my mother's makeup. She is tightly controlled, reserved, very proper and tough as hell. She is opposed to drinking, frivolity, and vice of any kind. There are rules of decency that must be obeyed. I have heard many stories of the early years of my parents' marriage, and I've lived through many tumultuous ones myself. My father is a life-of-the-party sort of guy who assumed that his young wife, so long as she had a nice home with nice things in it, would be content if he continued on as though she was not there. My mother had different ideas. After a few months of my father going out and carousing with his buddies and then wandering home at whatever time he liked, my mother changed the locks. Gutsy for a newly married twenty-one-year-old Arab woman. Off my dad went to get his father, Emile, who would come back, apologize to my mother on behalf of his errant son, lecture my dad on how my mother was too good for him, and obtain my mother's grudging forgiveness. This scene was played out a number of times. My mother was not going to be sidelined, which was a bit of a surprise for my dad. Those were rocky years while my mother staked her ground, but my father ultimately acquiesced to the new world order.

My father has a nickname for my mother: the Liquor Control Board. He is a firm believer in fun. She is a firm believer in not having fun. She has very fixed views about respectable behaviour, and being jovial and outgoing do not fall into that category. Apparently, the apple does not fall far from the tree. For years I chastised her about not being fun-loving, and yet my own children have taken to calling me the Director of Funland Security.

The truth is, my parents, who have been married over fifty years, have absolutely nothing in common. My mother always says, "If your father likes it, you know I won't, and vice versa." Fight night at the Henein household usually required me, from a very young age, to broker a truce between my parents and shield Pete from the fight. The fights were always over silly things, but the larger issue was incompatibility. Numerous times early on in their marriage, she up and left and went home to her mother only to return a day later.

There is only one thing they agree on—marriage requires sacrifice and commitment to your children. Their core familial values are perfectly aligned. This made their incompatibility tolerable and, indeed, the family sustainable. They never lost sight of this central, shared priority.

But this does not make for the most fulfilling existence. If my mother was not dealing with my brother and me or my father, she was entirely focused on her own mother. Teta had a very strong grip over my mother, and this was a constant source of resentment for my dad, who understandably wanted and should have had some of his wife's attention as well. My mother, however, sees all things as obligations—to her children, her husband, her mother. And she was going to meet every single obligation if it killed her. This is not unusual in Middle Eastern culture, where the expectation is that a daughter will always be devoted to and available for her parents. Culturally, the daughter bears most of the responsibilities, and it was no different in my family. If my mother had any free time, she would spend it with Teta. Any independent life outside the family was unimaginable, not to mention frowned upon. Something as simple as going out to dinner with her husband would be unacceptable unless my grandmother was there too, and so my mother never developed any friendships of her own. I do not recall my parents even once going to a movie or having dinner alone. Their friend group, and the social life that goes with it, grew only after we kids had left home and my grandparents had passed away.

Once all family obligations and distractions were behind them, my parents had to deal with each other. And they have. They've developed that rhythm that two people who have lived over half a century together do. There is something admirable and charmingly old-fashioned in that. I think there is a brief window of freedom for women like my mother when their children have left the nest and their husband is still working. My mom joined a book club, started making friends, became a real estate agent, and developed her own life outside the home. Then my dad retired. When men retire, often their external world shrinks. My mother had a new charge and all the responsibilities that went with it.

I am closer to my mother than she was to Teta, but in some respects our relationship mirrors theirs. I spend a great deal of time with her. I feel an obligation to take care of my parents. Rarely does a weekend go by when we are not together, either at home or travelling. Still, one thing differs in our respective relationships. My Teta dug in and held on to my mother for dear life. She would not let her go. My father fought for his stake and we children demanded ours. My mother, on the other hand, has repeatedly pushed me out and into the world without her. This is her true strength and her gift to me. She was adamant that coming to North America was an opportunity to make sure that I did not have to walk the same path that she did, that I did not have her constraints, and that the expectations and aspirations for me would be the same as those for a man. For her, North America was a real chance for equality for her daughter. So never at any point in my life did she say I was working too hard, that I needed to be home more, that I should feel any guilt for putting myself and my career first. Ultimately, her message to me was that I'm entitled to live in the world in a way she did not. If I walk unapologetically, it is because she insisted on no less.

The truth is that my mother did not want to get married. Although she voices no regrets, given another option she would have put marriage on hold and experienced a little more life. She has over the years done a lot of thinking on this subject and has even developed creative theories about rewriting the marriage contract. My favourite one opts for a ten-year term of licence where, at the ten-year mark, all marriages should presumptively dissolve with no penalty to either party. Her system allows for a five-year contractual renewal for good behaviour. Like parole. No marriage, she declares, should be a presumptive life sentence. This way, Mom says, not only do you get the option of opting out, but the threat of non-renewal acts as an incentive for each party to be on their best behaviour.

Considering her own experience, my getting married was not a big goal for my mother, much less a topic of discussion. I recall coming home from law school once after learning that there was something called a hope chest, a collection of household items such as china and linens that a mother apparently collects for her daughter and presents to her when she gets married. Why, I asked naively, was this custom, this demonstration of marital aspiration for one's daughter, non-existent in my family? Wrong question. My mother explained that she didn't raise me to get married. She saw her role as my mother to prepare me not for marriage but for independence. "When you are a lawyer," she ended her lecture, "you can buy whatever china and pots you want."

My very unscientific theory on marriage is that those who want to get married often don't find the right partner, and those who aren't ready often do. I did find the right partner, despite my not looking and the fact that, at twenty-nine, I was convinced I was far too young to be tying the knot. Both my mother and I were completely unprepared for my wedding, although the idea of planning a massive party where I would be the centre of attention was irresistible. That's the whole point of a wedding, right?

I insisted on going to New York to buy my dress. As Mom and I went from store to store being subjected to fluffy white princess dresses, I decided that I should get married in a black gown. This of course terrified my mother-in-law, who until the moment I walked down the aisle was trying to figure out how she could explain to her family why her daughter-in-law chose a black wedding dress. We were in a bridal store when a very lovely attendant looked at my mom and said, "This is such a special moment for you. Your princess is getting married. You should be very proud." I held my breath. "No," my mom responded, "I am not *proud* of my daughter because she is getting married. I was proud of her when she graduated from law school. I was even more proud of her when she got her master's degree at Columbia. I am not *proud* that she is getting married. I think you mean am I happy for her, and yes, I am, if this is what makes her happy." Mic drop. We didn't buy the dress.

We eventually did find one, though, a white version of something Morticia Addams might wear. It arrived the day before the wedding and had to be taken apart at the seams because it did not fit, so there was no time to try on the tailored version before the ceremony. My shoes came the day of. I had also not budgeted any time to write vows. Fortunately, my husband Glen and my cousin Hoda were tasked to write them. They were handed to me just before I walked down the aisle. I'd worried that they wouldn't be sufficiently strident, feminist, independent enough, but they were. And when we got to the "for richer or poorer" part, as I looked at my earnest husband's face, I could do nothing but laugh. I thought, *Poor Glen, you have no clue what you're signing up for.* "Poor Glen" became the theme of the wedding speeches.

For all my mother's strength in supporting my brother and me, it frustrated me that she never did more for herself, wasn't a little tougher or more demanding in her own life. There were years when I was resentful about this. How could she be such a staunch feminist, so determined to ensure my independence, and yet not fight like hell for her own? I don't know at what moment I finally realized that my parents were human, but I think it was then that I grew up.

The hour after my brother Pete and I fell asleep, before my dad got home from work, must have been the only moments my mother had to herself while we were growing up. I wonder now what she thought about, sitting alone in the quiet. Was it worth it, the trek to North America, the upheaval? Did her life turn out the way she had hoped, pouring everything into her children? Now she would say yes. But I don't think back then she wasted time thinking about it. Maybe because so little was her choice. That's how I see it. But that is not how she sees it. She chose to stay in her marriage. She chose the type of life she would live and make for her children. She would probably say that, when given the opportunity to choose, the decisions were all hers and they were right for her.

There is something admirable in her singularity of purpose, the sheer resolve and confidence she has that her choices were the right ones for her at that time and in those circumstances. My mother never second-guessed herself. No guilt. No regret. Unapologetic.

Because she was. And is.

6

HAVE A HOLLY, JOLLY POLYESTER CHRISTMAS

I'M NOT A NATURAL WHEN it comes to babies. During prenatal classes, my husband was the overenthusiastic new parent who expertly diapered and burped the baby doll. Every time he tried to hand me the doll, I refused. Naturally, all the moms-to-be cooed over him, and the dads-to-be were dazzled by his dexterity and ease with a pretend newborn. I was just bored, but, to be fair, I had warned him that babies weren't my thing and I would not participate in a class, even a pre-natal one, unless we were being marked and I could get an A. As a young girl, I hadn't liked playing with dolls unless it was to cut their hair and restyle them. After they were reimagined to my satisfaction, I forgot all about them. Once my mother bought me a baby boy doll that turned out to be anatomically correct in the most rudimentary way. I was so shocked, I never picked up another doll in my entire childhood. I didn't ask for them as gifts, and I never wanted to play house, never wanted a baby carriage or a pretend baby anything. And as I got older, I never quite got the fuss about babies; I think adults are far more interesting. They can actually talk. So I don't know why I was so excited about the birth of my brother, Peter, six years my junior. It was completely out of character.

My lack of enthusiasm about children is entirely my mother's fault. She's not a massive fan either. My mother was quite satisfied with one child. She had a stillbirth before me. Eight months into her first pregnancy, the baby stopped moving. My mom, twenty-three years old, was told that she would simply have to wait until she went into labour naturally. For four weeks, she carried around her dead child, a daughter. After the birth, my mother did not want to see her and rarely spoke of it again. A little over a year later, I was born. I think my mom was satisfied that she had suitably performed her familial duty, notwithstanding that she had failed to produce a male. My father didn't care a whole lot about that anyway, and he too was satisfied with our small family. It was Teta who found having one child simply unacceptable. She nagged my mother for years about having a second child, saying it was cruel to leave me without a sibling. As with all things that Teta demanded, my mom ultimately acquiesced.

The day Mom went into labour was the first day of my dad's new job at a pharmacy two hours from where we lived. Dad doesn't get taken off course easily, and not even the birth of his second child would divert him from his job. He told my mother to call Teta, and off he went to work. Several hours later, the chubbiest baby I've ever seen was born. Pete weighed in at a whopping ten and a half pounds. He was a naturally smiley baby with a wonderful disposition. But at two months he started to rapidly lose weight. He couldn't keep any food down and soon dropped back to his birth weight. My parents took him to doctor after doctor with no results, until one day, through a recommendation from a pharmacist my father knew, they were referred to a pediatrician who quickly diagnosed my brother with pyloric stenosis, an unusual condition that blocks food from entering the small intestine. My mom was told to take him to the hospital immediately, and emergency surgery was scheduled for that evening. She couldn't bring herself to stay there while it was being performed, telling Teta that he shouldn't have been given to her if he was going to be taken away so soon. My mom is strong in many ways, but she could not bear the thought of losing another child. Dad waited alone at the hospital. The surgery was successful, and my baby brother was sent home healed and healthy.

From the moment Pete came home, we were inseparable. While my mother was busy managing the house, getting through her day, I was largely left to mind my brother. I insisted that he learn the alphabet before he started kindergarten, so I made him sit through daily, often painstaking lessons. I would buy workbooks and make him complete the exercises. I became utterly preoccupied with the idea that he, Canadian born, needed to experience every single North American "thing" I could find, although my brother would likely say that I *subjected* him to every single North American thing I could find. And nothing expressed sisterly love like my maniacal obsession that Pete have the most perfect North American Christmas.

The parameters of an *Amerikani* Christmas were mysterious to me. I knew little more than what I saw on the relentless cycle of television cartoons. It certainly *seemed* magical. To this day, I can't make it through *Frosty the Snowman* without getting overwhelmed when he melts. And when the dog in *The Grinch Who Stole Christmas* starts perilously pulling that heaping sled down the mountain, the devastation of the moment requires me to leave the room. Christmas cartoons make me cry. Which, I admit, is a bit odd for a person who has spent almost three decades with her head deeply buried in things far worse than a cartoon dog with a heavy sled. Just when I get a grip, the goddamn Whos start singing the Whoville Christmas song. *Fahoo fores, dahoo dores.*

Christmas triggers a measure of holiday hysteria in me. In my younger years, I was known to make homemade wrapping paper or paint my own Martha Stewart Christmas ornaments until two in the morning. Pete is far more blasé about the season. I am convinced that is entirely attributable to the holiday festivities I inflicted on him while we were growing up. He has Yuletide post-traumatic stress disorder.

Every year, I knew that the Christmas season had officially begun when Mom descended into the bowels of our wood-panelled basement, flipped on the disco lights, and soon emerged with a dusty box containing our artificial Christmas tree. She would assemble it in the exact same spot every year, in front of the fake fireplace in our family room. Dad was always working, so he was completely uninvolved in anything Christmasy. Year after year, Mom put up the tree and did all the other Christmas rituals solo. The tree was nothing more than thin wire covered in badly fabricated plastic needles. Each year after the holidays, Mom would remove the branches and carefully place them in plastic bags she had labelled "A" through "F" so the branches didn't get mixed up. The plastic bag alphabetization method, however, was not foolproof. Invariably, an "A" branch found its way into a "D" bag, resulting the next year in a lopsided tree that looked as if it had been assembled upside down. And every year, once the errant branch was discovered, a full dismantling and reassembly was required. Understandably, with each branch reinsertion, Mom's mood got blacker. Once assembled, the plastic tree would be drenched in Brite Star silver tinsel. This was where Pete and I jumped in. Piece by piece, strand by strand, the tinsel icicles were applied with precision to the tree, and at the end of Christmas season they were removed strand by strand and stored in an old cardboard glove box. Mom was not going to spend another $1.99 on tinsel if she could help it.

Navigating the emotionally treacherous minefields of Christmas cartoons was bad enough for me, but trying to make sense of all the Christmas traditions was too much to ask. The government really should give out some sort of *Christmas for Dummies* book with citizenship papers. Mincemeat pie that has no meat in it. A drink made with eggs and alcohol and thick as syrup. Wine that is heated and served with cinnamon. Going to strangers' houses to sing to cheer them up. It was a lot of holiday cheer to take in for people who were stunned by the mere idea of snow.

The Christmas culinary and decorative demands were unforgiving. In pre–Martha Stewart days we had no one to guide us through the season. When I finally figured out that

North Americans "stuff" their turkeys, I insisted my family do away with Arabic food at Christmastime so we could have a *real* Christmas. Teta actually acquiesced but couldn't help stuffing the bird with rice, ground beef, and pine nuts because that is what everything is stuffed with in the Middle East. She made a *mahshi* turkey. *Mahshi* literally translates as "stuffed" and covers a wide range of Arabic food groups. A Christmas turkey would be afforded no different treatment than a zucchini. It was a principled position on Teta's part.

Every year at Christmastime, the Ice Capades would roll into town. Think of the Ice Capades as Siegfried and Roy on skates—glitter and sparkle in spandex on ice. This was a *real* Christmas experience, and when I was twelve I decided Pete needed to be a part of it. I just needed to get my mom to see it that way. After sufficient whining mixed with arguing the case that each and every child in North America must be taken to the Ice Capades to experience a true Christmas, my mother relented. I promised that all I wanted for Christmas that year was to take Pete to the Ice Capades.

Pete was the sweetest and gentlest six-year-old soul you could ever imagine. His only flaw was that he had no interest at all in the Ice Capades. But I had enough for both of us. Off the three of us went to downtown Toronto (Dad, of course, was working), Pete swathed from head to toe in a snowsuit, boots, a hat, and scarf. To this day, my mom insists that all children must be bundled up within an inch of their life to resist the winter cold. If your child is able to breathe comfortably, then you are a negligent parent for not properly suffocating them with warmth.

I hadn't told my mom that the real reason behind my demand that we get front-row tickets was that if you were really, really lucky, a giant skating bear would pick you to sit in a train that was wheeled around the ice for the big finale. And so the moment came. The skaters whizzed around looking for youngsters to ride the train. I, of course, was beside myself with anticipation verging on hysteria. I was committed to getting my family literally and figuratively on that North American train. I sat up straight, waved, pointed spastically to my brother to get the skaters' attention. And then it happened: they skated over and selected Pete. I shoved him into the giant skating bear's arms and off he went with him. My mom was impressed, since the selection of one of her children was obviously a clear and very public acknowledgment of her superior mothering skills and the quality of the children she had raised. The look of terror on Pete's face as he was carried away in the bear's arms didn't dampen her pleasure at all. Nor mine. Sure, he cried the whole time, but I was beaming. Pete was having a real North American Christmas—whether he liked it or not. I knew in my heart that he would thank me for this awesome experience as soon as the trauma had passed.

Traumatizing my brother with things that were in my view good for him became a favourite pastime for me. He would say that I still do this. Pete's forbearance of my intensity is extraordinary.

The plastic tree was also the harbinger of our yearly Christmas trek to the mall. Pete and I were suitably outfitted in head-to-toe polyester. Fortunately, nobody was tweeting, posting, sharing, or Instagramming anything in those days. If they'd tried, the phone would have exploded as the polyester-filled images were transmitted at lightning speed. Dressing appropriately for the Santa photo that was going to be sent to Egypt was an objective sign of our success in Canada. One particular Christmas, the outfits my mom put us in were glorious in their flammable polyesterness. The pants, stiff, with flared legs, made a fabulous scratching noise with every step I took up the stairs to reach Santa. My brother was equally dashing in a mustard-browny poo-coloured pair of pants, North Star running shoes, and striped shirt. And as we climbed up high on the mall Santa's knee, year after year, my brother always had that same exact look: completely amazed, flabbergasted really, that Santa Claus had actually come to the mall. Again. Just to see him. And my mother? Well, she could not have been more proud. Because as Pete and I sat there on Santa's lap, she knew. Her children had finally become real Canadians.

From a very young age, my role in the family was to wade into all familial confrontation, but I was always extremely protective of Pete. In my effort to distract him, we whiled away many nights with a small slide projector, watching cartoons on the wall. Pete and I have very different recollections of those early years. Even as a four-year-old, his natural instinct was to diffuse and distract with humour. He would spend hours telling my dad jokes to lighten the mood and entertain. Even when he was very young, his stand-up routines came fast and furious, his natural artistic bent always on display. He is unquestionably the funnier and smarter one of us. While I isolated myself for hours studying, Pete would crack jokes while doing his homework at the kitchen table, finishing in half the time and still being an A student.

We attended the same elementary school, but then for high school I went to the girls-only St. Joseph's Morrow Park and he went to the mirror Catholic school for boys. It took a while for Pete to find his place in the testosterone-filled hierarchy that is a boys' school, but eventually the blunt-force bullies of the group grew past their prime and those with some intellect came to the fore. For my brother, that did not happen until grade eleven, when he was cast as a lead in the school play. For three years, he was the lead in all the school plays. He is a natural star. He went from the shy, pushed-around kid to lead actor to graduating-class valedictorian. But that's my brother. Pete always does things on his own time and on his own terms.

When he went to the University of Toronto, he focused on English and, of course, theatre. As in high school, Mom and I went to every play, including the four-hour production of *Hamlet* with four different Hamlets in the seminal role. Pete graduated with honours, picked up his diploma on graduation day, handed it to my parents and said, "Here you go, this is for you, I'm done." And that was that. Try as my mother might to persuade him to continue school, Pete said he was off to pursue his true passion, acting. My artistic brother remains an enigma to both my mother and my father. I am the traditional immigrant kid—straight line, school, family, profession. My parents were not prepared for the diversion with Pete, the only one of us born on North American soil.

And so for the next six years, Pete pursued acting. He auditioned for a renowned theatre company in New York, Circle in the Square, and was offered a scholarship to study there. But he declined—he decided he wasn't ready to live in New York and wasn't committed to acting as a career. Instead, he moved to his true passion, comedy. When he first told me he was going to make the switch to comedy, I tried to dissuade him. There was no question he was funny, but a career comic required something else. Comedy is a rough, hard knock field. He rightly ignored me.

I've always been fascinated by comics—their quickness and intellect is self-evident. The lifestyle is gruelling, and exposing yourself on a stage to an often hostile audience takes nerves of steel. Comics are in their own heads most of the time, working out bits over and over again, except for the few minutes onstage when they come alive. That was Pete. If he could live onstage, he would. It is where he became a different person. He loved the audience, the interaction, the danger of not knowing what is coming next.

To suggest that my mother did not take this six-year interlude well would be a gross understatement. She could not believe that her son did not have, as she always said, a "respectable" profession. One day Pete announced he was going to try busking. When he explained that this was singing in the street (he is multitalented), my mother burst into tears and said, "My son is not going to be a beggar." And so for many of those six years, Mom would call me, after a sleepless night worrying, distressed about how Pete would make a living or how he could ever support himself, let alone a family. I insisted that he be allowed to follow his true passion. My parents had refused to allow me to take a year off during law school to travel, so I was adamant that Pete would have the freedom to take the path he wanted. The arguments between Mom and me went on for the entire six years. Pete, meanwhile, remained largely unmoved. He can be profoundly resolute that way.

Six years into his career, a variety show that was being shot in Hollywood was looking to hire a full-time comedian on the show, and Pete was asked to fly to Hollywood to audition. But the audition coincided with a planned trip to England with his soon-to-be wife. Pete agonized over it. I insisted that he go, offered to reschedule the flights, said I would pay for everything because this was clearly his big break. After two weeks of excuse after excuse, as we were walking down the street together he told me he had decided to pass. I lost it. I am sure I could be heard ten blocks away. I can't fully explain why I took his decision so personally, but I did. Six years of his struggle, six years of family fighting, and he had decided he was out. It is, to this day, the biggest fight we've ever had.

For two months we did not talk. In my family, fighting is as routine as apple pie, but not talking is an unacceptable aberration. For siblings who had talked to each other virtually every day of our lives, that two months was a long and serious fracture. My mother and father eventually interceded because a fractured family was intolerable to them. So with my father's cajoling and my mom's expressions of disappointment at our behaviour, we started talking again.

During our first conversation, Pete said he had made a decision. The artistic life, he told me, was neither practical nor sufficiently fulfilling. He was going to law school. And he did. He graduated with flying colours and landed a job at a large downtown law firm where he eventually became a partner. He is, of course, a litigator, and an extremely talented one at that. Which makes sense. The court is just a slightly modified stage. He feels at home there too.

We have been inseparable since his birth. He is the one person who can make me laugh no matter what crisis I'm going through, and our juvenile behaviour when we are together invariably annoys our mother. On one of my parents' anniversaries, we took them out for a fancy dinner. While my mom waxed on about how proud she was of her two children, *respectable* lawyers, Pete and I tried to hang spoons from our noses and told inappropriate jokes, causing her to call us badly behaved animals and then storm off. She refused to have dinner with us for months. She still talks about our bad behaviour that night.

For years, I was Pete's confidante far more than my mother. I was his go-to person. But in every relationship—parental, sibling, or friendship—there is always an undulation, a wave in the dynamic. And for us, as we have grown older, Peter has become my confidant and one of my greatest supports. I call him for advice because I know that he is one of the few people who has my back like no other. He more than anyone has lifted me through the darkest moments in the purest way. He knows me and my cadence. He often intercedes to explain me to others when I simply cannot explain myself, he can rationalize all of me—he does not see the dissonance so many assume. He runs me through my closing arguments to a jury, hears me go through my cross-examinations, and makes my speeches much funnier than I ever could make them.

I was asked to do a stand-up routine for a charity function. Initially I said no because I could not think of anything more terrifying. Being funny is not exactly what I am known for. That's my brother's zone, not mine. But after staring at the invite for months, I called the organizer and said I would do it because I could not think of anything that terrified me more. The organizer told me not to worry, I would be assigned a coach. But I told him that the only reason I'd agreed is that I already had one. And so over the next month, Pete and I scripted my routine, and he ran me through it for days. He would show me how to perform it. And every day, I would tell him it really would be much better if he could just do it for me. I was that terrified. On the day of the performance, as I walked onto the stage (actually I was carried by four drag queens, because a girl's gotta make an entrance), Pete was sitting off to the side of the stage, routine in hand, within my eyesight. He was more nervous for me than I was.

My father has this annoying habit. Throughout my life, he frequently calls me by his sister's name, Renée. And for years, I'd get angry and ask how it was that he could not keep his daughter and sister straight. He would always say, "It is because I love my sister so much that I call my daughter by her name." I constantly call my oldest son Pete. My son knows why the names are interchangeable for me. He is far more gracious than I ever was.

7

LOOK AT THE LIGHTS, AREN'T THEY PRETTY?

"STOP EATING YOUR WORDS, start again," my father would say as he made me read out loud to him. This one thing he would make me practise over and over again. On Sundays, my father's day off, he would listen to me read, learning to enunciate, to speak publicly, as though he knew that I would need this one day.

At least some of my father's DNA is palpable in me. We are both academically and professionally disciplined. No matter how mundane the task, we have the capacity to grind it out for as long as it takes; put us on a hamster wheel and we will spin endlessly. My father's stamina is exemplified by his approach to a profession that was neither his dream nor suitable to his personality. I'd hear him every morning at six, rustling in the kitchen making a cup of thick, pungent Turkish coffee. After this morning ritual and reading the newspaper, he would drive to work in a rough part of town to stand behind a pharmaceutical dispensary for twelve hours a day, six days a week for most of his career. He would come home at nine thirty, eat his dinner alone in the kitchen and fall asleep on the floor, regaling us with a symphony of snoring until my mom nudged him awake to go to bed. And then up he'd get the next day and do it all over again, year after year after year. On the occasional vacation to Florida, all he would want to do was soak up the sun and have a couple of Scotches—nothing fancy, just the cheapest Johnnie Walker. Once back home he was at it again. He did this without ever complaining.

I don't remember having dinner with my father until I was about sixteen, and whenever I griped about this to my mother, she would snap, "Your father is working." End of discussion. I worked for him one summer, and I know what his days looked like. For a man who had an active mind, thrived on good verbal sparring, and loved meeting people and socializing, being a pharmacist was a stifling choice of profession.

His optimism must have contributed to his stamina. My father is a pathological optimist, to the point of denying even undeniable bad news. In high school I was scalded on my leg by boiling water and refused to go to the hospital because I was in the middle of studying for an exam. Don't ask. I'm obsessive this way. Dad was adamant it was nothing that some Ozonol couldn't fix. After my exam, my mom insisted on taking me to the doctor because the skin had bubbled and blackened. I had second-degree burns that required the skin to be removed and daily dressings administered. My father couldn't stand to look at it, and to this day I tease him about Ozonol as a cure-all. His own eventual cancer, as well as my mother's, he managed with the same optimism. When I press him, he always says, "Why get upset over things you cannot control?" He likes to keep things upbeat until bad news is unavoidable. It is a frustrating trait for the rest of us who, true to our Middle Eastern roots, feel that bad news can only be borne if it is thinned out by spreading a layer of it over your nearest and dearest. It is much easier to share misery.

I have his discipline, the ability to do something I dislike continuously because I have to. Not in my profession, mind you—that fulfills me intellectually and emotionally. My obsession was performing academically even though I rarely enjoyed it. But the wheel had to keep spinning. How else can you explain my refusal to leave our hotel room on a family trip so that I could complete an utterly inconsequential high school essay on Keats's "Ode on a Grecian Urn"? I finally emerged on the last day to get into the ocean just to calm my father down. He could not fathom that he had worked hard to take his family to the beach and I had yet to get into the ocean. An unconscionable and inexplicable crime. He was right. The beach would have been a far more productive experience than the essay. That story still frustrates my father. The only arguments my mother and I had about school were those where she asked me to stop studying. She would fight with me to take a break or come eat or join a family gathering. I missed many such events—even my grandmother's mandatory weekend family dinners—because I insisted on studying just a little bit longer. And the thing is that I never, not once, enjoyed it. I played piano for ten years, an instrument I had absolutely no interest in, because quitting was not an option. This comes solely from my father, this capacity to be single-minded, obstinate, shoulder to the wheel. The difference between us is that while we both spin, my father stares straight ahead, whereas I try to figure out where there is another, bigger, shinier, more exciting wheel to reduce boredom.

There are other undeniable similarities. Our interest in politics, our love of arguing over anything, the desire to out-match each other in any debate, the love of literature. Being more persuasive than the other is sport for us. And had my dad been given the opportunity, I have no doubt he would have been a great advocate or politician. His impassioned plea in defence of one of our dogs who had done something or other he shouldn't have rivals any closing argument I have made. If my dad could have spent his life pleading death-penalty cases, imploring people to be human and humane, he would have done it beautifully, cajoling, charming. He has a natural curiosity about people and never fails to elicit the cab driver's life story, the waiter's job aspirations, the clerk's political leanings. He knew every one of his regular customers' life stories—their origins, their troubles, all about their children— and they would always greet him like a long-lost family member. But though my father is an extrovert in this way, he never made real friends in this country, never established any lasting relationships with all the people he interacted with. I thought it had to do with the disconnection he felt upon leaving Egypt and the friends he had there, but now I think I am wrong. It is not his natural curiosity about people at all that drives this part of him, but rather the sport of asking questions, of consuming information about people. Maybe that is where I get the need for compulsive information gathering— why cross-examination is the easiest conversation for me to have. It must feed some part of us.

My father recognizes some of himself in me and is proud of those similarities. But the things that he is most proud of are entirely unpredictable, like my winning a frozen turkey in a Thanksgiving lottery at the local supermarket when I was eleven years old. "We went to the store and Marie was allowed to pick the largest frozen turkey of all," he says as though this lottery win was an expression of skill on my part, a predictor of future success. It is rivalled perhaps only by a trip he and I took to the local exhibition, where I won an obscene number of stuffed animals. He forgets the first part, why we went at all—he and Mom had a fight, and in a fit of anger he took me to the exhibition just to get out of the house—but he describes the haul in detail, always ending the story with the fact that we were able to get all the animals for only $175, which in 1975 was a heck of a lot of money. I think he did it just as an act of defiance to my fiscally oppressive mom. My mother was and is unimpressed. These stories, each of which involved external validation—the frozen turkey, the stuffed pink dogs—were, as far as my dad is concerned, indicative of the superior Henein DNA.

For my father, what other people say makes one's success in this country real, tangible. For the longest time, not quite understanding what my professional achievements were exactly, he would react with delight if a stranger complimented him about me. The external validation was key for him, prompting my mother to get annoyed and say, "Obviously *my* daughter is talented." I'm not sure he quite believed it, not until recently anyway. There is a disconnection between the person he reads about in the paper and his daughter. To this day, he likes to report to me the details he has read about a case of mine as though he is speaking to a stranger. And every time, when I remind him that I know what happened in court because *I* was, in fact, the lawyer asking the questions in the courtroom that day, he always looks surprised, as though it had not occurred to him that I might know something about the case that the newspapers are reporting. The lawyer and his daughter are two different people, not readily reconciled. "A real Henein," he says when he recounts the frozen turkey story, but not when he recounts a story of me the lawyer.

Recently, however, he has taken pride in seeing the family name in the media or being asked about me. Now he proudly responds, "She is my daughter." And every time, he is surprised that a stranger would ask a question about me. And every time, he reports the conversation with the same sense of bewilderment and pride. I once received flowers from my father after I'd won a big case. My dad was not one to get us gifts or cards; that was always Mom's job. He had written on the card: "Your fame is so well, well deserved. I am so, so proud of you. Words cannot express it. Love, Dad." I know the words were his.

"We see our family name in the paper in this country because of you," he said to me recently.

"That is why I told you I would never change my last name," I say. He nods, and I know exactly what he is thinking. *The move to this country was right.*

But there are aspects of my character whose origins I cannot trace, that I know do not come from my father. My chronic restlessness, for example, is the opposite of his need for ritual and repetition. The second time that I have to do anything is one time too many. This is why I do not understand my friends who go to the same cottage every weekend, go to the same club, or insist on eating at the same restaurant over and over again. I find it painful, even soul crushing, to have the same experience more than a couple of times. I cannot even bear to drive the same route home from my office for one week straight. I am always changing it up for no reason other than the repetition is too much for me. I don't know what I expect to find when I turn left rather than right, but at least I've changed the scenery and sometimes I think I might see something that I wouldn't have seen otherwise. My constant need to see something new, anything new, is inexplicable to my father and certainly not a Henein trait.

My hardness, for lack of a better term, is another thing I cannot trace to either of my parents, or any relatives for that matter. It has been part of me for as long as I remember. I believe it is at least part of the reason for my professional success, but it is equally the reason for my most significant failings. My mother was not giving me a compliment when, during an argument when I was twelve, she glared at me and said, "You are very hard, Marie." My friends—many successful, strong women—invariably come to the same conclusion. Sometimes I think they're saying I am uncompromising, unforgiving, and other times I think they actually intend it as a compliment, that I am tough and strong. Eddie Greenspan said I was one of the toughest people he knew, and I know he meant that this was a good quality, at least as far as my career was concerned. While it has served me well in my work, and before that in academics, in other ways it has not. It can make me unforgiving and hard to satisfy. It takes conscious effort on my part to move past an initial unempathetic reaction. Empathy is not my go-to move. Fortunately, I am surrounded by people for whom it is and they nudge me along the way. This has caused me to force myself to at least become more controlled and deliberate. To take a breath and rethink. To always do a gut check so that when I do respond, particularly in court, I have thought it all through and I am confident in my response or approach. I am generally in control. Interestingly, having that control has been the positive byproduct of a not so positive personality trait.

I have known I can be hard for as long as I remember. Since elementary school, I have repeatedly been told to be *softer*, less tough, and more *female*. I can't. It isn't in me. I received the first of many warnings to this effect in grade seven, when, in an attempt at model politics, my class had chosen a president who would preside over weekly meetings.

His name was Billy and he was completely inoffensive, and, in my unfair view, utterly ineffective. To me, this was evidenced by his failure to equitably monitor the use of the basketball net in the schoolyard. It became apparent that only the cool boys and girls were given access to the net, which in my grade seven mind was an injustice of epic proportion. Let me just confess that I did not, and do not, play basketball—not then, not now, not ever. I hate sports. In fact, I am the least athletic human you will ever meet, and yet this schoolyard unfairness was untenable for me. And so, during one of our class parliamentary discussions, I challenged President Billy on this. After I called him out, I proceeded to itemize his complete absence of leadership qualities. It was unnecessarily mean of me. He cried and ran out of the class. I should've felt bad. I didn't. I enjoyed the verbal beat down.

This was not how my male teacher saw it. He took me for a walk and explained that being diplomatic was very important for a girl. Apparently, I cannot make other people cry. I had no clue what he was talking about. It would take me another thirty years to figure out how to be more restrained, more controlled and let something go occasionally. That same teacher inscribed a novel I was reading "To the next Donna Summer," which was odd since I can't sing. Maybe the inscription should have been "To the next prime minister." But that was probably saved for Billy, not the girl who'd made him cry.

That certainly wasn't the only time I would be lectured on how to behave like a nice girl. In high school, I was again pulled aside by a male teacher and told that I needed to be softer; otherwise, men would not listen to me. There were boys who did not invite me to the prom because I was not feminine enough. Whatever "softer" meant, the fact is I was

not capable of it, and did not aspire to it. And quite frankly, my parents and my friends didn't advocate for it. So there it is. I am good with this hardness, to be honest. It is who I am and who I have always been; the edges have been sanded off by virtue of age and experience and the need for some diplomacy in certain situations, but the edge is always there. I haven't changed much—just added a little more control. It's just that I'd like to figure out where it came from and I can't.

Originally, I thought perhaps this toughness came from my father's line, although his family still remains a mystery to me in a way that my mother's does not. Dad's relatives only made cameo appearances while I was growing up, flitting in and out of our life, never setting down any sort of roots. They remained largely in Egypt. When the holidays came, my dad was often sad that they were not with him, so much so that some Christmases he returned to Egypt to visit his brother, sister, and father. We never accompanied him on those trips. He had no interest in taking us home, and my mother had no interest in sending *her* children there. In fact, the one and only time I went to Cairo was not with my father but with my mother and Teta, when I was in my early twenties.

Yet I am told that I take after the Henein women. The story goes that my father's aunts and cousins in Cairo did not fit the traditional mould of Middle Eastern women. They got married as they were required to do, but through some misadventure or other—a husband who couldn't keep a job or who died young— many of these women found themselves left alone to support their families and themselves. At a time when wives and mothers cooked, cleaned, and took care of children inside the home, these women worked outside the home, successfully ran businesses, and had careers. "They were the men of the house," my mom says, with more than a hint of admiration. I have not heard anyone from my father's side of the family speak of them with any interest, except to say that I take after them. The men's stories are told with great pride, but the women were relegated to a footnote unless it was to extol their virtues as mothers and cooks.

Who were these women? I know one was a comedienne, another a business owner. My mother says she's never met any of these mythical Henein women. The first one I came to know was my father's sister, Renée, or Renno as she was called. Had she grown up in North America, Renée—who was voluptuous, like a Middle Eastern Sophia Loren—would have surely been scooped up by Hollywood. She is a romantic who likes the attention of men and being flattered, and at the age of fifteen she fell in love with a military man and insisted on marrying him. But her teenage sweetheart turned out to be a brute. Each time she fled him, she would run back to her mother, who in turn would send her back to her husband. Try as he might, my father could not persuade her to leave him. That was understandable, given the time and place. Once married in Egypt, as in many countries, a woman is ruined, unusable for anyone who comes along next. There was no viable life beyond her first husband. To this day in the Middle East, after their husbands die or divorce them, women don't remarry or happily carry on. To do so would be viewed as a breach of character. I know many Middle Eastern women who find the thought of moving on from a deceased or divorced husband unconscionable, and Renée was no different.

After twenty years, Renée's husband announced that he had fallen in love with someone else and unceremoniously left my aunt. He suffered no social retribution as a result, no public isolation, disapproval, or limitation whatsoever. Everyone assumed my aunt must have done something to cause her husband to leave—too headstrong, too mouthy, too friendly. However you filled in the blank, the calculus was the same: the failure was my aunt's, not his. During their long separation, Renée enjoyed some freedom but struggled. In the absence of a formal divorce, Egyptian law gave her husband dominion over most of her financial affairs and even her movements. Her husband actually had control over her passport so that she could not travel out of the country without his permission.

Twenty more years came and went. My aunt, who was a successful seamstress, was fortunately able to earn enough money to support herself, and eventually her husband relented on the passport. And then one day, as quickly as he had left, he returned, not because he had come to his senses and done the decent thing, but because the woman he'd run off with had died and he needed someone to take care of him. Renée took him back without hesitation.

My aunt would steal little bits of reprieve from him when she came to stay with us for a few weeks every now and then.

That is when I came to know her, when she was already in her seventies. Even at that age, she had a singsong voice and loved nothing more than a good off-colour joke. Invariably, the two of us would have the same conversation.

"Why did you take him back?"

"I had no choice," she would say. "It was hard in Egypt, without a man, to get around, to go out to live a life. I wasn't allowed."

"But *why*?" I'd ask.

She would laugh her gravelly laugh and say it again: "Because I had no choice."

I was young then and could not see her resilience or strength. I am ashamed to say that the forbearance of women was viewed by me sometimes as a weakness. It is not. This quiet fortitude is at the core of our strength and resilience, but it takes maturity to see that. Back then, after yet another one of these conversations with Renée, I was left disappointed, not understanding what Henein women my mother had imagined. Whoever they were, I was quite sure they were not like my aunt Renée. Where was *I* in this equation? Then I met my first cousin, Hoda.

My father's brother, Saad, had a miserable, unpleasant marriage, but he was able to succeed in having two wonderful children—Hoda, who is one year older than I, and Milo, who is my brother's age. While we were mirror images in family composition, that was where the similarities ended. Hoda's mother, after back-and-forth breakups and get-togethers, had moved with Hoda's father to Sacramento. With us living in faraway Toronto, as a child I only had the chance to meet Hoda once, when I was twelve. I remember taking her to the CN Tower and, of course, to the mall because Arabs always take visiting relatives to the mall. We didn't talk much, other than me saying how much I admired a necklace she was wearing.

It was a stoplight with a ruby for red, emerald for green and a topaz for yellow. Hoda immediately took it off and gave it to me. That pretty much sums up Hoda. She will unquestioningly give you anything she has. Her capacity for kindness exceeds that of anyone I have ever known.

Hoda's mother eventually left my uncle and moved to New York City with her children. Hoda was gone again after the one trip to Toronto, even though our families were only an hour away by plane. My uncle forbade my family from having anything to do with his ex-wife or his children. Any contact was viewed as an act of disloyalty. We are tribal in this regard. There is a well-known saying among us: *I against my brothers. I and my brothers against my cousins. I and my brothers and my cousins against the world.* So, because of our solidarity with my uncle, Hoda disappeared from my life as suddenly as she had come into it. I knew nothing about her growing up, what she did for a living, or exactly where in New York she lived.

It was while I was at Columbia Law School that my mother told me Hoda lived close by. Mom had tracked down Hoda's mom in Queens and arranged a visit. Not long after, we headed there to meet up, and then waited for Hoda to arrive. After some time, Hoda swanned in late, because, as I would learn, my cousin lives on a clock that runs at least two hours later than anyone else's. A short person with wildly curly black hair came in, larger than life, saying she was sorry she was late but she had just finished her shift driving a limo for some famous actor whose name I can't remember. She was warm and friendly, but like me she was guarded, because in between us were years of unspoken family history. That first meeting was a little uncomfortable. I couldn't figure her out, and the feeling was mutual. Mom and I left after a couple of hours. Hoda being Hoda, which is gracious and welcoming to her core, got in touch with me after my mother had returned to Toronto and started inviting me to family gatherings. And I went. I had no one else to be with.

At first we didn't know how to get to know each other. Our complicated family history would always interfere. She was angry at her father; I was defensive of mine. She would take me out on the town after a chauffuring gig, picking me up in her limo and tour me through the city like a tourist. We would drive to Lincoln Center and she would say, "Look at the lights, aren't they pretty?" It was as though she had no connection to me. I might as well have been just any stranger being toured around the city in a limo. To this day we say to each other, "Look at the lights, aren't they pretty?" It is code between us for *You're blowing me off*.

Clearly, if we wanted to get along, we needed to figure out the terms of engagement—and one day we did. We agreed that we would get to know each other without the intercession of any family history. We would simply never discuss it. It would be just her and me. We would connect or not. So on 2 a.m. treks through Little Italy or long, late conversations over Chinese food, we slowly came to know each other. Once the family baggage was removed, we realized that we were connected. She was the mythical Henein woman I had been told about. In Hoda, I had found a part of me.

We were both born into Middle Eastern families, but our paths quickly diverged. My parents were fixed on integrating into North American life, while Hoda's went the opposite route and clung with everything they had to their Arab ways. Whereas my family took to eating out regularly at Crock & Block, Steak n' Burger, Mother's Pizza, and, best of all,

Whaler's Wharf, Hoda and her family enveloped themselves in all things Middle Eastern. Not a weekend went by that did not involve Hoda and her family getting together with her seemingly million distant cousins and uncles and aunts. Her large and thoroughly Middle Eastern family continued to be at the core of everything—unlike mine. There was no dispersion, no unmooring from old ways. Arabic music was played, Arabic was spoken, and Middle Eastern food was all that was eaten. Hoda embraced this part of her culture and still does. Her children—half Irish—also embrace their roots, and although they do not speak Arabic, they are grounded in that culture in a way my children are not. Nor are my brother and I.

Like my father, Hoda cannot walk into a restaurant, a hotel lobby, anywhere in the world without getting to know the people she interacts with. But unlike my father, Hoda goes the next step. Once she knows their life story, their troubles, then she insists on helping. I have lost count of how many people she has adopted. It is not unusual for me to call only for her to say something like she is just taking her aunt Dorothy to the hospital. *You don't have an aunt Dorothy,* I say. *Well no, she's not my real aunt but I met her a few months ago and she has no one to take care of her so I'm doing it.* Hoda collects people not to surround herself with them but because she needs to help. She is like my father's mother in that way. Kind to strangers, always willing to help everyone and anyone.

Hoda's maternal uncle stepped in to fill the void that her father had left. He was the one to walk Hoda down the aisle, to fly down and sit outside the courtroom during her divorce proceedings, and she has been by his side during his fight with cancer. They are inseparable and connected. Hoda and I talk about their relationship, the closeness, the fact that he is always in her corner and lets her be who she wants to be without judgment. And then it occurs to me. Separated, worlds apart, he is her Sami. In every way. Her family, like mine, doesn't discuss his sexuality, but unlike mine, there is at least a quiet acceptance of who he truly is.

We are connected in this way and more. Over the last twenty-five years, we have been through births and deaths and divorces together. If one needs the other, we know and immediately call or text. We can go weeks not talking and then know it is time. We argue about who is tougher. Who is moodier. We lay alternate claim to those titles depending on the particular day. And I cannot imagine life without her. As Hoda likes to remind me, she is one of the few people who can put me in my place. Hoda and my oldest hold that spot like nobody else.

She knows me in a way that cannot be explained by friendship, that can only be explained by the fact that our origin is in some way inextricably woven together, that we come from the same stock. She knows me in a way that people who come from the same place know each other. It is comforting. And yet there are things that even we cannot reconcile. Whenever we argue, and we must, Hoda always says to me, "You are too hard, too unforgiving." "What do you mean?" I ask. "*You know*," she says.

And I do. That is the truth. Some things are just your own. There is no origin. Just you.

MIDDLES

8

MARIA GOES TO WORK

I KNEW WHAT I WAS signing up for when I chose this profession. Criminal law is not a nine-to-five job. Nor is it work that you can easily balance with other parts of your life. Maybe someone out there has the fortitude to accomplish the high-wire juggling act of doing it all, but that person is not me. It is a crisis management job. Nobody is at their highpoint when they are sitting in my office or in a witness stand. After spending the day reviewing autopsy pictures or hearing the distress of clients, I found it hard to go home, get on the floor and cheerfully play Lego with my kids.

Even when I think I am compartmentalizing, I'm really not. The people closest to me pay the price when the work seeps out despite my best attempts to contain it. My oldest and I have a bit of a routine. Exasperated in the midst of an argument, he says "I'd like to speak to Marie *my mom*, not Marie *the lawyer*." He's right, as usual. I always respond by reminding him that the problem is that his mom and the lawyer are one and the same. We do this dance often, he and I, with no resolution. Unfortunately, my family gets a bit of both of me, and some-times more of one than the other. *Stop cross-examining me, stop trying to win an argument as though you're in court. Can't we just have a conversation?* Truth is, sometimes, I cannot.

Law students often ask me what has been the greatest sac-rifice in my legal career. The answer is obvious. Be prepared to give up a significant part of yourself. You will not leave the pro-fession the same way you came in. It's not possible. All of us who work in criminal justice—prosecutors, defence lawyers, judges, journalists, police officers—pay the same price. It's impossible to breathe in a good dose of toxicity, desperation, and pain in the courtroom halls and think your lungs can stay clean. Breathing easily gives way to an intensity I find hard to let go of. Everything gives way. Family, pleasure, your personality, all those essential parts of you get cannibalized. On most days, I wouldn't change a thing; I love the work that much.

A lawyer's road into a courtroom is a long, academic one. After a three- or four-year undergraduate degree and three more years of law school, there is the mandatory year of apprenticeship called articling. Law school was not exactly what I thought it was going to be. I entered law school at the tender age of twenty-one. I had just come back from backpacking through Europe with my friend, Rita. We stopped en route home in London, where I fell in love with the punk scene. The first day in law school, I arrived with long hair, stiletto nails, a silver fringed leather jacket, and leopard print pointy shoes. The other students asked if I was visiting from the art school. Clearly, I didn't quite fit in. That never changed. I had no interest in the corporate firms, the big money, or the competitiveness of it all. I had come for criminal law, nothing else. I often tell students who ask my advice not to be as single-minded as I was. It is a significant commitment to make at twenty-one with no life experience.

I had imagined that law school was going to be full of like-minded people and professors that taught through the Socratic method. Maybe I had been watching too much television, my singular reference point for law school and lawyers. There were certainly some professors who tried to spark students, but it was hard for me to get outraged over the injustice of real estate law. And to see injustice in family law, property law, contracts, labour law—because the reality is the inequities and injustices are everywhere you look in law—takes some maturity and world experience. I entered law school with neither of those things.

The academics I could figure out. It was becoming a real lawyer that would take me time. Law school does not prepare us for the profession in many respects. Just as the transition from working on cadavers to living human beings must take some adjusting after medical school. In law school, it is all about deconstructing a case that is over. The decision has been made and this is a post-game analysis. As a law student, you naturally spend a great deal of time learning the law, much of which has completely changed by the time you graduate and ever get a chance to litigate anything. The constitutional law that I learned in law school, for example, was the Charter in its infancy, and it has transformed immeasurably in the last thirty years. The first ten years of Charter litigation involved some of the most critical work done on defining the scope of our rights and constitutional interpretation. But thirty years later, much of it has changed. The law is never stagnant. But law school basics, are necessary. You must first understand what exists, why we are where we are in the law to know when the moment is ripe to change it or push it in a different direction. Often, it takes several cracks at a legal principle before the legal system is prepared to rethink it. Enthusiasm, right thinking, activism, good sentiments are not enough without a strong academic grounding.

The real value in law school is that it teaches students how to think critically and analytically. Critical thinking is not as reflexive as you may first believe. Think of how effective social media misinformation has been—so effective that it has been easily weaponized by nation states. The battlefield has moved from land mines to the minds of citizens. It is not the medium that is at fault, it is the consumer. Our human nature makes us sitting ducks. We are prepared to believe most things as long as they align with our preconceptions or predispositions. Law school challenges this reflex and makes you a critical, some might say cynical, thinker. Navigating a case effectively requires an ability to critically think, set aside your ego, and most importantly, challenge your own and your client's assumptions.

While law school does some of this, it completely fails to teach students about the actual practice of law. Very little time is spent on how to interact with clients, tackle ethical issues, or master the art of negotiation and advocacy. There are a

smattering of courses here and there on the curriculum that give a passing nod to these skills, but most of us graduate without any substantial training in litigation or negotiation. That essential training happens during articling year and in places where there isn't this mandatory year of apprenticeship, during the first few years of practice.

Having gotten to the top rung of the educational ladder, an articling student is once again dropped to the very bottom of the legal hierarchy. Law is a hierarchical profession, and earning your stripes is just part of the trip. Notwithstanding the complete absence of any world experience, young lawyers often start their first year bubbling over with unearned and misplaced self-confidence. As Oscar Wilde is reputed to have said, "I am not young enough to know everything." Age disabuses you of that unbridled arrogance.

I was that young once, just on the cusp of twenty-four when I started articling and my law education really began. The true purpose of the articling process is a lesson in humility, something not normally associated with twenty-somethings. The first five years of any lawyer's career after articling are focused on breaking down the novice and building up a real lawyer in their place. You cannot start learning how to practise law until you've come to terms with how little you know. Over the years, experience teaches good lawyers the humility to always do a gut check and second-guess themselves. The best lawyers I know have the humility to do that re-evaluation and settle on a course of action in a case only after they've exhausted other views and opinions. Surprisingly, senior lawyers do more consulting with each other than young lawyers because at that late stage, they appreciate the significance of every single decision they make in the life of a case. Nothing is inconsequential.

I didn't know any of that coming out of law school, but I did know two things with crystal clarity: that I wanted to be a criminal defence lawyer, and where I wanted to work. When Eddie Greenspan's autobiography, *Greenspan: The Case for the Defence*, was published in 1987, I was still in law school. That Christmas, I lost count of how many copies of the book I received from friends and family; it was no secret that I admired him. Whenever I was asked what I hoped to do after law school, I would always say that it was to work with Eddie Greenspan. To me, he was the quintessential criminal defence lawyer, 100 percent pure, undiluted, and quirky as all hell. A cross between Clarence Darrow and Rumpole of the Bailey, he seemed to have stepped right out of central casting. Eddie was exactly what I imagined a criminal lawyer was. And what I wanted to be. In that office, every win and every single loss was personal. If I ever needed someone to fight for me, he would've been it.

When it came time to apply for articling positions, I applied to only seven or eight criminal defence firms. No big fancy mega-law firms for me, the kind that spend obscene amounts of money wining and dining students only to either show them the door before they make partner or have half the women running for the hills long before that. Nor did I apply to the prosecutor's office that advertised itself as the largest law firm in the country. I have done some prosecution work in the regulatory law context and am confident that I'm the only prosecutor to have received a thank-you card from the person she is prosecuting. It is just not in my makeup. I knew exactly what I wanted even at twenty-four. Explaining the decision to my parents, I told them that if I did not get an articling job at a criminal defence firm, I would have to quit law and start over with another career. My parents had no clue how the legal business worked, but they knew enough to be alarmed, especially my father, who is averse to stepping out of any predictable linear career path. Go to school, get a job, work, retire. Throwing it all away because I couldn't follow my passion was inexplicable to him.

My dream, of course, was to article for Eddie, but my interview was with one of his partners, who seemed wholly uninterested in talking to me. I offered to show him a piece of my writing and he politely declined. He didn't ask me a single question. I get it now, but back then I had no clue how irrelevant I was to the whole operation. I would add zero value to the firm other than to provide a warm body to do basic work. I left the interview devastated, convinced I would never get my dream job. On the day that offers were to be made, I sat in the kitchen by the phone desperately waiting for *the* call (yes, the phone was stuck to the wall). And it finally came. I was offered a one-year articling position at Eddie's firm.

My parents breathed a sigh of relief, now having tangible proof that their trip across the ocean had not been for nothing. Their daughter was going to be a lawyer *and* working at a prestigious firm. My mother was beside herself for a different reason. I was on the road to being financially independent. *You are no different from a man*, my mother's lullaby, that she thankfully continued to whisper to me over the next several years as I started to build my career.

I was not worried about being able to do the work. It was what I was going to wear that was stressing me out. I gave it an unnecessary and inordinate amount of thought. Fashion figures prominently in many of my important life decisions. It is a distraction and escape. As one friend says, my IQ drops like a stone the minute I walk into a clothing store. Consistent with this vapidity, and in a bit of utterly meaningless conscientious objection, I refused to wear the typical lawyer's blue suit to article, although someone should probably have pointed out that no one was going to notice me at all, much less what I was wearing. Eschewing the blue-suit uniform, which just wasn't me anyway, I went to my first day of work in a Norma Kamali beige blazer and black pencil skirt with, of course, towering heels. My mother had bought the jacket and skirt for me as a present for my articling inter-views. It was the first time that we had ever been in a designer store, and the prices caused her to choke. I explained that this purchase was absolutely necessary to my professional success, and that if I didn't nail my first sartorial impression, I was doomed to be in a blue suit and practical shoes for the rest of my days—a thought almost as untenable as not practising criminal law. I was prepared to work non-stop every day at my job, I just wasn't about to do it in sensible shoes.

There was no welcome package, no office meeting, no introduction to my duties when I arrived at the office. That's just not the way things were done at that firm. I learned that my articling partner had quit after only two weeks on the job. I have absolutely no clue what the real reason was, but I was told that he was disinclined to work on such mundane matters as frauds and wanted to only do murder cases. He was apparently a blood-and-guts type and had drawn his proverbial line in the sand. Fair enough.

I had no such line. I was willing to do anything and everything, from photocopying and personally delivering documents all over the city to drafting motions and trial preparation. Prima donnas were not welcome in that office, most especially if they were articling students. You did what you had to do to get the job done for the client. If that meant writing a brief for the Supreme Court of Canada, then photocopying the thousands of pages of the casebook and then driving it to the airport yourself at six in the morning so it got to the Supreme Court in Ottawa on time, then that is exactly what you did. That is what I did—photocopying, binding, typing my own dictation because there was no assistant to assist, driving briefs to couriers more than once. And if it meant getting Eddie's car cleaned, picking up his laundry, or driving to Cambridge, Ontario, to pick up butter tarts, well that too was part of the job.

Eddie wasn't looking for indentured servitude but rather for an unwavering commitment to the work and the office to the exclusion of everything else. He believed a real lawyer could not be precious. You roll up your sleeves and dig in. I was a more than willing participant. My family in those years gave up on expecting me to attend most family events, including holidays. I trudged off to a jail to see a new client on New Year's Day, and I was on the phone at all hours. One day I had to go and see a murder client at the Cobourg jail, and my dad decided to accompany me for the ride. I told him he could stay in the prison waiting room until I was through. When I came out from seeing the client, my dad's face was white. He didn't know that lawyers sit in a small room with their clients without any security, and he confessed that for the hour he was waiting, he was worried sick about me. Another time, my mother received a call telling her that I had been kidnapped. When she called the office to tell them about the call, the response was unfazed. They assured her I would show up sooner or later. Despite these small scares, my family was supportive of me, although I am sure somedays they wondered why I hadn't picked a "nicer" area of the law to practise.

Eddie's office was on the top floor of a downtown tower, an unusually luxurious location for a criminal law firm. Those office locations were reserved for mega-firms with a long lineage. Criminal lawyers are not usually included in the lunching, clubbing, white collar crowd. That first week, I wandered the halls looking for work and waited for the moment when I would get an introduction to the namesake of the firm. It happened towards the end of the second week. I was at my desk at eleven thirty at night when I received a call. I instantly knew who it was from the gruff, gravelly voice.

"Who are you?" he asked.

"Marie. I'm your new articling student, Mr. Greenspan."

"All right, Marie, tell me who's at the office."

And that was my introduction—no "welcome to the firm" and certainly no small talk, but roll call to determine who was putting enough hours in. Over the years, I would try various diversionary tactics to draw Eddie's attention away from the 11:30 PM roll call. *Who do you want to speak to? Can I help with something?* Nothing worked. Trying to distract someone who is an expert at asking questions was a waste of time. I came to expect those late-night calls. It was either roll call or discussing a case on his drive home or talking about some great new restaurant he'd read about. And some nights, at 11:30, you'd hear him walking down the hall, jangling the change in his pocket and muttering, "Nobody works here anymore." He could not understand why anybody would ever want to be anywhere else.

For weeks I called him Mr. Greenspan, even though everyone else called him Eddie. Knowing my place, I waited for Mr. Greenspan to invite me to address him by his first name. When, after a while, I asked his long-time assistant when that day was coming, she laughed and said, "That day is never coming. Just call him Eddie." And so I did. That was Eddie. He wasn't going to make it easy on you, whether you were a witness or an employee. Your ease was not his priority. You had to earn his respect. This was classic old-school apprenticeship.

My own name was a whole other matter. For some reason, around the office and even in court, I was always referred to, both in transcripts and verbally, as Maria. Eddie noticed it too. The two of us started saving all the correspondence and judgments that called me Maria Henein. How hard could it be to spell *Marie*? I'm convinced it wasn't the spelling that was confounding. It was my appearance. Long black hair. Dark features. *Where are you really from, Maria?* As though I should be sweeping the floor rather than litigating. Eddie got that my name mattered to me. He understood being an outsider, as a Jewish lawyer from a small town in a profession of legacy. He was an outsider through and through. That is what made him a fierce opponent—he wasn't trying to be liked or invited golfing. And so it became our little joke. He would call me Maria—but only to me and never in front of anyone else. He knew the meaning of a name—of *my* name.

After I finished articling for the firm, I applied to graduate school. I had asked Eddie what I should do, stay with the office or go off to do my master's. He told me that if I left, they could not hold a position for me. But he also advised that it would be foolish to pass up the opportunity. If it were him, he would go. And so I went to Columbia University to obtain a master of laws.

Living in New York had long been my goal, but when I finally got there, I was not ready. I had no family or friends for support. Most importantly, I had no Sami, and it was difficult to get my bearings. Just as with the first day of school, my grandmother travelled with me by train and stayed to help me settle in. Teta and I tried to find the places Sami would take us, but we couldn't. My parents took turns coming to visit me each month to keep my spirits up. Each time, my father left in tears that he was leaving me. Each time, my mother told me to toughen up.

When I returned to Toronto, I had neither a job nor any prospects. For the first time in my life, I felt at a professional loss, completely directionless. It would have helped if I actually applied for a job, but I did not. I didn't send out a single résumé. I do not know whether this was from inertia or fatigue, but I came to a full stop at that time in my life. I had been going full tilt for as long as I could remember, and I guess I just ran out of steam. I couldn't clearly see the next move. Fortunately, a criminal law professor I had worked for as a research assistant knew I was back and got in touch with me. My first year in law school had been Alan Young's first year teaching. He was, to say the least, an unconventional professor, Harvard educated, Supreme Court clerk, a red-haired hippie who was uncompromisingly committed to individual liberty and opposed to any form of morality law. He is a brilliant legal mind who spearheaded challenges to the prostitution laws in Canada as well as the legalization of marijuana. When I returned from Columbia Law School, he happened to be working on an appeal relating to a marijuana grow operation and needed some assistance. I took him up on the offer. Co-counsel was Marc Rosenberg, Eddie's partner, and so I found myself back in the office where I had articled. One day, while I was doing some photocopying, Eddie sauntered in and asked me if I wanted to come back and work for him—a no-frills-Eddie job offer. Without a second thought I said yes. It was where I would remain for over a decade.

Eddie was a character, larger than life, the epitome of the classic criminal barrister. He was dynamic, complex, wickedly funny, and obsessed with criminal law. Eddie approached the law and all legal analysis with the fundamental view that if the law is not as it should be, if it is unfair, then our job as lawyers was to figure out how to correct it, and then how to challenge it.

My job, for many of the years that I was in that office, was not to litigate my own cases but rather to junior as "second chair" to Eddie. This involved preparing the trial and going to court but not doing the majority of the actual litigating. I would be given a file and expected to work it up, which included everything from interviewing clients to chasing down witnesses to preparing legal motions. Shortly before

the trial—often the night before—Eddie would summon me for the trial prep session. To describe him as a quick study doesn't quite capture it. Usually, these trial prep sessions happened as he was splayed out on the couch in his office. He would order me to read aloud the legal memos or all the witness statements. Meanwhile he'd seemingly float in and out of a state of semi-consciousness, sometimes even falling asleep and snoring. And when I got up to tiptoe out of the office, thinking he had not heard a thing I'd said, he would rouse like a bear from a winter slumber, often making similar sounds, and ask the one essential question or focus on the one aspect that was at the absolute heart of the case. He had taken it all in, thought about it and knew exactly where to go. He would invariably ask me about the one thing I hadn't thought to do. "Have you gone to the scene?" Any lawyer worth their salt knows you must. "Have you considered this legal argument?" I hadn't. It became a game. How close could I come to not missing something that he would spot even in a state of half slumber? He was that good.

That is the greatest gift of a natural litigator. In basketball, they talk about a player's ability to "see the court." A player who can see the court sees the entirety of the game and the plays three moves down the line. Eddie could see the court. He could see the heart of the case, the theory, and the weakness intuitively. He was three moves ahead. No amount of training can give you that. That is pure instinct.

For the next several years, my work–life balance in that office was work, no life. Work was what I did, from morning till night and on weekends. Days did not seem to end. At some point during our preparation sessions, Eddie would get tired or bored and I would often drive him home, only to be summoned back to his house at five or six in the morning to continue where we'd left off. Weekends were workdays with marginally more flexible hours. The office was always full and buzzing on Sundays. One week I decided to go home a little early, at around seven thirty or eight. That ended when Eddie's partner pulled me into his office and gently explained that people who really wanted to work in that office did not leave early.

Eddie himself virtually lived in the office. It was his home. He was there early in the morning, would stay until dinnertime, when he would usually cross the street to his favourite Italian restaurant or meet some friends at a nearby deli, and then come back at eleven ready to work again. I spent countless evenings waiting for Eddie to return from dinner because he'd said he would be back to prepare, only to get a phone call from him around midnight telling me he was too tired and had gone home—or not receive a phone call at all. Waiting for Eddie was just part of the job.

There were moments of downtime, of course. Eddie had a wicked sense of humour, and hours would be spent in his office at the end of the day, all of us congregating on his couch and talking about everything law, food, travel, and gossip. If a student had nothing to do, Eddie would dispatch them on a two-hour drive outside the city to get what he said were the best butter tarts in Canada. Other days, we would spend until the early-morning hours preparing a cross-examination, and then after court we'd celebrate by going to Eddie's favourite diner and ordering every pie on the menu. It was intense, unrelenting, a grind—and exhilarating.

However, it was what happened in the courtroom, the culmination of all this hard work and unrelenting long hours, that was special. When you watch a flawless cross-examination that appears fluid or seamless or even extemporaneous, this is deceiving. What you are witnessing is the very end product of a process that often takes months; a process that involves agonizing over each and every question, every word or phrase, every point of the cross-examination, so that the cross-examination is effective. Because of the amount of control Eddie had over a cross-examination, he made it look too easy to most observers. But I had more than a front-row seat. I knew exactly what had gone into preparing those cross-examinations—the strategy, the work, the stress in trying to establish where it would begin and how it would crescendo—constructing it layer upon layer. What happened in the courtroom, the control, was the final step.

John Henry Wigmore, a legendary American legal theorist, called cross-examination "the greatest engine of truth." But it is a poor weapon compared with what an accused is up against. Given the power of a police force, given all the investigative tools and funds that the state has at its disposal, cross-examination is like bringing a knife to a gun fight—you are significantly outpowered. When I hear people say that the accused has all the rights, I often wonder what I'm missing. If by "all the rights" they mean the presumption of innocence and the burden of proof, then that is true. But those protections pale against the power of the government when it has directed its considerable arsenal at you for prosecution.

In a nutshell, cross-examination, this great engine of truth, is the ability to ask questions and to control the wording and order of those questions. That is all. The theory is that through cross-examination, the truth will be magically revealed. There are many days that I ask myself, is that all I've got? But contrary to what you see on *Law and Order* or read in legal thrillers, it is not a shoot-from-the-hip exercise. In a real courtroom, there are very few of those "gotcha" moments. In reality, it is a painstaking, methodical grind to mount an effective cross-examination. But in the end, it is usually all we have.

Through skilful cross-examination, a lawyer may be able to unfold their client's theory or reveal a lie in a witness's evidence. But no matter how many books are written about the art of cross-examination—and there are thousands—the one thing that cannot be taught is the understanding of human nature that must accompany any successful cross-examination. It is imperative to have a clear perception of who the witness is and where the weaknesses lie in them and their testimony. The cross-examiner must be able to understand the witness's nature. We generally do not have access to the other side's witnesses, who are often understandably antagonistic or do not wish to speak with the defence. We try to *understand* the witness by thinking through our theory of the case, the Crown's theory, the possible motivation for the witness to say things, who they are, and what their story really is. As lawyers, we need to do this to be able to know who we are meeting in court often for the very first time. Cross-examination is a fluid and surprisingly organic process. You must have more than one speed; you have to be able to adjust in the moment with the type of witness you are dealing with. And often the same witness is many different people during one cross-examination.

I would often watch Eddie in court and realize that, done correctly, cross-examination can mean the difference between conviction and acquittal. There were so many examples of Eddie's genius, his pure instinct, but one in particular stands out for me. Eddie had finished cross-examining a witness early, and we had not expected the Crown to call the second witness to the stand. We were unprepared and had not re-worked the cross. In a panic, Eddie asked me to hand him the witness's CV. He looked it over for a few moments and noticed that there was a gap in the schooling. And that is where he started—something seemingly inconsequential that, by the end of one hour of cross-examination solely on this history and résumé, had the witness admitting to perjury no fewer than seven times.

I learned more about being an effective lawyer in those years as a second chair to Eddie than any amount of litigation of my own cases could ever have taught me. And there was a moment about ten years into the job when I watched Eddie in court and I thought to myself, I am ready to do this on my own. I felt that I had enough confidence to make the essential judgment calls that are necessary in the art of litigation. I fig-ured it would take me a decade to get comfortable in my job and another decade to really hone my skills. But I'm getting ahead of myself.

There was another side to my relationship with Eddie. It was temperamental. He was moody, and I certainly kept pace. We worked well together, but it usually involved a good deal of arguing back and forth until the right course of action had been agreed upon. Given my Middle Eastern tempera-ment, our disputes could often be spirited, to put it mildly, but they never became personal. In so many respects I was fortunate to land where I did. Eddie's firm was the right place for me because he in particular did not try to soften the edges or expect me to be more "ladylike" or less tough. Eddie viewed toughness as an asset in a lawyer. He let me enter and develop in this profession on my own terms and critically, in my own skin. And that was absolutely essential to my survival in this career. I had moved from a home where I was told I was no different from a man to an office that lived by the same rule. Eddie personally understood being an outsider: he himself had been a Jewish upstart in a profession that was run by WASPs. The legal profession's doors were generally closed to many of us. And if you had not noticed that doors were being knocked down, then you couldn't miss it when you entered the doors of his penthouse office.

Eddie was not the only star in the firm. His partner was the widely esteemed Marc Rosenberg. Later elevated to the Court of Appeal for Ontario, Marc was one of the greatest legal minds this country has ever known. He was an appellate lawyer who acted for people who had been convicted and were down to their last kick at the can in the justice system. For most clients, he was truly their final hope.

An appeal is very different from a trial. At a trial, both sides are allowed to call witnesses. But for the very rare exception, there is no witness on an appeal, and no cross-examination. Rather than a single judge or a judge and jury, an appellate court is generally composed of three judges. The argument proceeds first in writing, and then, under a tight time constraint, the lawyer presents an oral argument to persuade the court that a legal error was made in the trial court. In the Supreme Court of Canada, the highest appellate court in the country, nine judges usually hear cases, and no matter how important the case is to the country as a whole, each side gets no more than an hour to speak. In the United States, it is generally as little as twenty minutes.

Appellate advocacy is an entirely different art form of concentrated advocacy, and very few lawyers have mastered it. Marc was one of those lawyers. Still and quiet by nature, and without an ounce of ego, he was revered by judges, Crown attorneys, and defence lawyers alike. It was not unusual for a judge to call him for advice or a Crown or defence lawyer to call for guidance on a case. His court submissions were low-key, usually delivered with arms folded, one hand over his mouth. And everything he said sounded so eminently reasonable, as though it was not only the correct answer but the only answer that any right-thinking, decent person could have. He was pragmatic and had an ability to think through the most complex legal problems and simplify them. He made the answer the most obvious and clear-minded choice. There were no moral grey areas with Marc. Right and wrong were as clear to him as night and day. At the heart of his advocacy, the law had to be principled *and* humane. To watch Marc in court, you could not miss the respect and admiration that he was treated with, a credibility that can only be earned through genuineness.

But the singular quality that made Marc such an outstanding appellate lawyer was the objective judgment he brought to bear on a case. I recall writing an appeal for him about an infamous NHL fight that had ended with a player being criminally charged. Written with journalistic flair, my factum—the written legal argument submitted on appeal—was a work of wishful fiction. Marc retrieved the video of the fight, made me watch it with him and then asked me if what I had written reflected what I just saw. He was right. It did not.

A successful written argument is one that deals with all the facts in a scrupulously accurate manner. Effective advocacy is not about sleight of hand. I know trickery is what TV shows would have you believe. You give lawyers too much credit. We are not magicians and do not pull rabbits out of hats. You are rarely the smartest person in the room. Effective advocacy is about confronting the weaknesses in your case and overcoming them, which involves a combination of humility and rigour. One day in appeal court, while I railed at the questions the judges lobbed at me, confounded at how they did not understand (I hate when people disagree with me), Marc said that if the judges were not understanding my argument, it was because I had failed to convey it clearly. The fault was with me.

His advice changed the way I approached and argued appeals. What was at first blush an argument, a fight, became a conversation; a question from the bench became an opportunity to persuade rather than a personal challenge to be rebutted. The goal of any advocacy is, first, to be heard. If a judge does not want to listen to you, then you have already lost. A lawyer's credibility is why people listen and are prepared to be persuaded. If you do not have the first, you will not master the second. You have hobbled yourself right out of the starting gate. The court always listened to Eddie and Marc. They would lean forward and take in every word as though they were one of them.

Eddie's and Marc's offices were next to each other, connected, separated only by a bathroom and Eddie's small backroom. If Eddie was not in his office, odds were that he was sitting in Marc's ratty old blue velvet striped armchair or lying on a couch as they worked out a legal problem. Their relationship was symbiotic and one of mutual respect. Eddie thought the world of Marc's knowledge of the law and his skill as a craftsman of legal argument, and Marc was in awe of Eddie's trial skill and instinct. I wish every lawyer could have had the chance to sit in their offices, as I often did, and witness the two of them working together. It was a thing of beauty, a part of our Canadian legal history. I was often dispatched by Eddie to ask Marc a question or work through an issue Eddie had raised. And Marc was never dismissive of any of Eddie's ideas. For me, there was no answer that I gave Eddie that wouldn't be followed up by "Did you ask Marc if you're right?" If I did not have Marc's seal of approval, then I needed to get it—and this was true for everyone at the firm. Eddie and Marc were the perfect team.

I remained at Greenspan, Rosenberg & Buhr (which eventually became Greenspan, Henein & White) for the first eleven years of my career, in a professional environment that was rare. It was where my love of criminal law grew, surrounded by people who were as committed to the importance of the role of defence lawyers as they were to the justice system. We knew our ethical obligations and the extent and constraints of our role. That office was an office of professionals, not hired guns or mouth-pieces. I had landed in an environment that was a throwback—think of the lawyers depicted in *Inherit the Wind* or *To Kill a Mockingbird*—grounded in a complete absence of cynicism about what our profession does and the legal system in which we do it. Every single one of us loved criminal law—it was our profession, our hobby, what we fought and argued about in the office and during dinner, and what we talked about and thought about in our spare time. There was no off switch.

You can learn from every case, Eddie would say. Speak whenever you are invited because you never know who is in the audience. Do cases big and small, trial and appellate. Everything contributes to making you a better lawyer. That was Eddie's approach. Eddie would routinely take cases simply because they were interesting or the person needed help. We eventually decided that he shouldn't attend any initial client meetings, as any sob story suckered him and we would end up doing the case for next to nothing. Marc, too, spent much of his career arguing legal aid cases at the appellate court, cases that involved the most marginalized and indigent in our society. There is no question that we did a lot of high-paying work, but we also did a great deal of low- and no-paying work. All of it got the same attention and commitment.

When my colleague Alison Wheeler and I came up with the idea to provide pro bono appellate lawyers to unrepresented individuals at the Court of Appeal, Eddie said of course, even though it meant we would be doing free work several days a month. Marc, then a judge of the Court of Appeal, managed the program with us. The Pro Bono Inmate Appeals Program, now well into its second decade, continues to be staffed by appellate criminal lawyers who donate their time arguing cases for free in the Court of Appeal. These lawyers are unsung heroes, each and every one of them.

After over a decade working with Eddie, I was beginning to get surly. I was acting like a teenager itching to move out of her parents' house. I was annoyed at sitting second chair. And while now a partner at Greenspan, Henein and White, I was frustrated I had no control over the finances of a firm that had my name on it. I was unable to see how my future would play out. I did not like having to answer to Eddie anymore or being fully at his disposal. And I was often working six and sometimes seven days a week and rarely leaving the office before eleven at night. I was done, that's the truth. My inherent restlessness, which I had held in check all those years, had come back with a vengeance. In my gut, I knew it was time to try something different. It was time for me to leave and to pursue the dream of having my name, a woman's name, first on the letterhead, even if it turned out to be letterhead that no one would ever bother to read. I didn't care. Maria needed to go to work.

I told my husband that I was ready to leave, that I needed to know whether I could make it in this business on my own, with my own firm. I thought that an excellent time to do this was when we had a young child and had just bought a fixer-upper of a house that we could not afford, let alone renovate. I would be leaving with no clients of my own, and I had no idea where I might set up shop. I warned my husband that given my sparse attention to any financial planning, we would likely have to sell the house, as I wouldn't be earning an income for some time, if ever. I said I might end up in a strip mall working out of a storefront, but he didn't seem to care. This discussion happened over a single weekend—I was that eager to go.

I had no clue how Eddie would react when I told him I wanted to leave, and I wrestled with how to tell him. We had worked together closely for a long time, and I considered the office a second—and sometimes first—home. I had become a lawyer there. To me, leaving on terms that were respectful was the most important thing. So in the end I just came out with the truth. It was time for me to leave home; I needed to figure out what I was made of. I told him I had no plans, no office, and had not spoken to a single person about the decision other than my husband. It was not an easy conversation to have; these types of conversations never are. This was the only professional home I had ever known. After some discussion, Eddie asked me to stay for six months to transition cases, which I did. He gave me a few files to keep me going, the most important being a legal aid murder case involving an Israeli soldier, and that was that. On my last day I said goodbye and packed up all of my stuff, literally a decade in two boxes, and walked out the door.

I think a lot about Eddie and Marc all these years later. After I left the firm, whenever I had a question or a strategy I needed to work through, they were my first two calls. Eddie would immediately answer and spend as much time as I needed to tackle a problem. I didn't always follow his advice, but the process by which we arrived at the right path forward worked for me. Marc, too, continued to be my close friend, tolerating my outrage over the most recent appellate judgment, talking me off the professional ledge and being the most sober second thinker I have met next to my husband, who has that very same capacity for empathy and firm judgment. Years after I had left, I would often find myself automatically driving to Eddie's office rather than mine. My time at that firm, working with Eddie and Marc, was that indelibly impressed on my psyche.

I never imagined my career without their presence, yet not long after Marc retired from the Court of Appeal, he was diagnosed with a terminal illness. It was a long and painful decline. And while he was in the last phase of his illness, I received an email from one of his colleagues telling me that Eddie had suddenly passed away. I was in shock. Marc succumbed to his illness only a few months later.

Losing both of these friends and former colleagues was profoundly painful. When you lose people close to you, you do not lose that natural reflex to reach out to them, to speak to them as though they were still here, and it is always a bit jarring to remember they are not. As I manoeuvred through personally and legally complex cases, more than once I wished desperately that I could call on them for guidance. For a long time, I would pick up the phone to call one or the other of them only to remember that they were no longer there to answer. There were so many times that I truly forgot they were gone, had dialed their numbers, and then was struck with disbelief when I remembered.

Despite all those years of working so closely alongside Eddie, I never actually knew what he thought of me as a lawyer. That was just the way he was; he didn't exactly throw compliments around. I can recall him telling me only three things in that regard. Once, when I was still pretty junior, he told me I had a natural "trial instinct," and I was over the moon that he thought so. The second was after I had delivered a speech and Eddie said that I was untameable, completely incapable of toeing the party line. He knew me. And the third was telling me that he thought I had made it into the white, rather crusty male legal crowd on my own terms.

People are forever hunting for an explanation for women's success, as though we are all Pygmalions to be moulded. Eddie did not make me. He did not, I expect, spend any time at all thinking about my career, nor should he have. That was not his job and not his concern. What he did do is show me how to be a lawyer. He showed me how to fight and he showed me exactly the type of lawyer that I wanted to be. And for that, I am forever grateful.

In the back of Eddie's office, he had framed numerous articles that had been written about him over the years. And when he was not around, I would sneak in there and read those articles over and over again. One day, after I left the firm, Eddie called me to his office. He said that he had a gift for me and pulled out a frame. In it was an article written by Christie Blatchford, a well-known sharp-witted, sharp-tongued journalist who makes many people nervous, including lawyers. She was uncompromising and unsparing. She had written about a case of mine and called me "formidable." Eddie had highlighted that one word and framed the article for me.

It was the only gift he ever gave me. And it said everything I needed to hear from him.

9

DOES ANYBODY KNOW YOU'RE OUT THERE?

AFTER MORE THAN A DECADE of working in one of the top law firms in the country, I found myself starting from scratch. My mother thought that opening my own law firm was a great idea; my father not so much. I had no office space and very few clients. Also, I had no savings to pay myself, my assistant, or the young lawyer I had persuaded to join me. Most people would consider this overall lousy business planning, but I didn't care about the inherent uncertainty or the potential for failure. I figured the worst-case scenario was that we would have to sell our house and I would have to look for a job with an existing firm. And the best-case? Well, maybe I could manage to grow the firm by two or three lawyers.

I did have some very clear ideas about what I did not want to do. I knew that I did not want to be in the downtown core in a giant steel tower with windows that could not open. I would not spend my life going up and down in an elevator just to get a breath of fresh air or a coffee. So I found a brick-and-beam loft space with a colleague who was also looking for office space. More Google vibe than conventional stuffy law firm, it was far more space than I needed, but I signed the lease hoping to one day be able to fill my share of three offices.

With no money to pay either first or last month's rent, I had to borrow from my parents, promising I would pay them back as soon as I started earning some money. Next was trying to secure a small operating line of credit, something I was nervous about qualifying for, given our new mortgage, the complete absence of savings and the risk of the new business I proposed to start. Objectively, I was not a good bet for a bank lender, but without an operating line of credit there was no way I would be able to meet my basic monthly payments. I held my breath. Luckily I was approved for just enough credit to be able to pay my assistant and junior lawyer for a few months even if business was at a complete standstill. For the first few months, we worked at wooden fold-out tables rented from a party supply store until the leased furniture and computers started to arrive. Gradually, the place began to look like an actual law office.

I sat there every day waiting for the phone to ring. And every day, like clockwork, it did. But it wasn't clients calling, it was my father. Until that point in my life, my father had never picked up the phone to speak to me or my brother. He finds the phone a perplexing device. When we were growing up, every time it would ring at home, my dad, shocked, would turn to my mother demanding to know who could conceivably be calling, as though the caller were an intruder. He has never acclimated to the concept of a cell phone, although he has an old one that he keeps for emergencies. When he is forced to occasionally answer a phone call, he is profoundly awkward and stilted, as though he is not quite sure how a telephone works.

Notwithstanding his visceral aversion to telephones, when I opened my office, my father started calling me daily. And each and every day, the conversation between us was exactly the same.

"Marie, does anybody know you're out there?"

"I have no clue, Dad."

Silence. "Then how will clients know to call you? How will they find you?"

"I have no clue, Dad."

"Okay, talk to you tomorrow."

For months, this was the ritual, betraying my dad's tremendous anxiety that after all the effort to come to this country and give me a chance, I was making the greatest mistake of my life.

Unlike my father, I was not at all anxious about my somewhat capricious move. It felt right. For a person who is so disciplined, some might say obsessive, about many things, it is strange that most of my significant career decisions have been driven by nothing more than an instinct that it was the right move and the right time. The decision to start my own firm felt intuitively correct at that stage in my career. I was confident enough in my legal ability and decision making, and to me, that was the only thing that mattered. The rest of it, the *business* of law, would come or it would not. The only risk I cared about was whether I was ready to do my job effectively.

The truth is, I had no clue who knew I was out there in the sea of other lawyers. My career to date had been spent largely holed up in an office and junioring to Eddie and Marc. While I had been working hard and lecturing extensively, the one thing I had not done was spend any time learning how to market myself. I did not come from a familial line of lawyers—there was no legacy there—and frankly I was embarrassed to approach other lawyers and introduce myself. Criminal lawyers are notoriously awful at business development. That is partly the nature of the beast. Our business does not generally involve repeat clientele. Nor are we seasoned at doing business lunches. Our life is spent at the office or in court, and court days aren't exactly structured around strategic schmoozing: we grab a coffee and bagel on the run, not socialize at golf clubs. Add to that my own level of discomfort at lunching with someone for the sole purpose of selling myself, and I had no clue how to start.

I began attending the odd professional conference to try to pick up some helpful tips, and I even read a little about how to develop business in the legal profession. I read about taking people to lunch and telling them directly that you would like to work with them, sending out personalized thank-you notes if you got a referral, and sending holiday cards just to remind people that you are open for business. It was all foreign to me. I didn't send thank-you notes after my own wedding, so doing it in the context of a business transaction seemed more than a little out of character. But I tried, I truly did. I would write stilted notes—and then rewrite them because my handwriting is lousy. I would do uncomfortable "business" lunches and try to subtly sell myself, always being profoundly embarrassed.

None of this contributed one iota to whatever success I have had to date. I came to firmly believe that in the legal profession, at least at that stage of my career, business would come from one of two sources. The first was colleagues, lawyers who had seen me at work in court and believed I was competent at what I did. Lawyers tend to refer work to other lawyers in whom they have confidence. And the second source of work would be people I liked and was personally friendly with. This doesn't mean that I haven't worked with people who are not friends or who I am not particularly fond of, but as a rule, I try to avoid it.

Only a few principles guided my approach to developing my career: work hard, focus on my forensic skills, and develop friendships rather than "business" relationships. I'm not saying this is the only path to success. I have no clue what the right path to success is for any given person. I can only tell you what worked for me. What I came to figure out was that my so-called career strategy is based on my temperament, my personality, and the things that I prioritize. I will do numerous things I dislike over and over if I believe that the result will be worth the effort, but if I don't buy it, then I can't get behind it. And I didn't buy the trite play-it-safe, don't-be-yourself, appeal-to-everyone business-lunching wisdom of the blue-suit crowd. I didn't think the result was worth it, so I gave up whatever small attempt I'd made at trying to be someone I was not. That was not how I wanted to build my career or my firm.

I could spend time itemizing the highlights in our firm's development, or talk about our clients and their cases and the business of how our firm has gotten to where it is, but that's more
the stuff of the vanity publications that big and established law
firms publish on behalf of their legacy, and anyway, I believe
it is categorically the choice of our clients whether they want
to tell their stories or not. But here is what I can say, especially
as a female lawyer: there has been a lot of ink spilled about
my image and our firm's "branding". I can't figure out whether
people think I am or am not what they imagine a female
criminal lawyer should be. But something about me seems
to be confusing.

As my practice developed, the one thing that starting my
own firm let me do was create the type of working environment
that I wanted to be in daily, one that was more authentic to
me. No amount of branding or career planning can control the
many things that go into the trajectory of a career. My "image"
has not been remade, and by "image" I suspect most people
are talking about how I look. If you've read this far, you know
I have been obsessed with fashion since I was four years old and
playing dress-up with my uncle Sami. My family owned a fashion store, my grandmother was a seamstress, and my mother
has always been fixated on looking and being fashionable. I
have changed over the years, this is true. It is also true that
most of us do not look the same as we did when we were twenty
or thirty years old. I can assure you that in some ways I wish I
did. I went from shoulder-length hair to unruly, awful curly hair
post-baby to short punky hair. The latter is true to my somewhat gothy, punky inclinations. I discovered a straightening

iron, the greatest invention ever. I was able to afford more of the clothing that I liked, and I became less concerned about looking "lawyerly." My nails got longer and a little more outrageous. I always looked professional but I dressed in ways that made me more comfortable and that more closely reflected who I am despite being in this profession.

I feel the need to explain this because the view that my image is put on merely for some kind of effect—although I'm not sure what effect exactly—is inaccurate. It's not an "image"; it's *me*. It is what I choose to look like today but may not be what I want to look like a month from now. If I could be restyled, dressed up, made up and over every day, all day and shop full-time like it was my job, I probably would. For a little while, anyway. I find it entertaining and fun, nothing more. How I choose to look is not a business ploy. To think otherwise is asinine. Yet these sorts of questions are routinely directed not just at me but at women in whatever profession they're in, especially if the field is male-dominated. My male counterparts are never asked what they wear or what their image is. They do not have to explain their suit choice. Reporters do not comment on the style of their hair or the brand of their shoes. Clients retain lawyers who they are confident have their best interests at heart and can get results. They do not retain lawyers because of the length of their hair or what labels they are wearing. If I am trying to "say" anything about myself, it is not in the height of my heels that you will find the message; it is in my performance in and out of court on any given day. The result would be the same if I was in sweatpants and Birkenstocks.

My firm's "brand" has caused as much confusion as my appearance. I am frequently called by lawyers asking me who our brand or marketing manager is. I'm it. And the so-called brand grew and defined itself as we all did. Our great brand strategy usually involves me coming up with an idea driven largely by something utterly frivolous or that is annoying me, then sauntering into my partners' offices and saying, "I know this is crazy but I have an idea," and them saying yes to the whole thing. That is the extent of our brand management.

Ironically, the result of this haphazard brand management has resulted in a definitive brand. But it has always been organic, unplanned and, quite frankly, driven by something that I thought was funny. One year, I was getting annoyed by all the holiday e-cards that law firms were sending out. Each one was more sanctimonious than the other, completely removed from reality. Cards saying things like "What do you wish for this Holiday Season?" which then flipped to clips of lawyers expressing many wonderful and magnanimous thoughts for the world, completely and utterly disconnected from the business of law and the firm itself. Law, our profession, is a business. Most of us, the ones who send e-cards, are for-profit businesses, not charities. We are not generally saints and activists so sending out a card touting the charity your firm is supporting is just marketing. Make a donation and shut up about it. Don't sell your "wokeness" to clients. The cards annoyed me. I decided to hire a friend of a friend of a friend to help create our own video card. The first year's showed me walking through the office with the song "You're a Mean One, Mr. Grinch" playing as I knocked down Christmas trees, snapped gingerbread cookies and spat eggnog in an associate's face. The video ended with a message to have fun this holiday break. We didn't think much of the whole thing and sent it to our friends for a laugh. It created a good buzz we didn't expect.

When it came to updating the look of our website, which I had paid little attention to, the branding was similarly organic. My sister-in-law, who works in bookkeeping in the advertising industry, introduced me to a friend who owned an ad company. He agreed, as a favour and at a huge discount, to help us out. His firm marketed products like chips and pop, not lawyers, and they had no clue what we really did or what message we wanted to convey. We had no idea about messaging either. They presented us with options for photographers. I chose the ones who did fashion photography, for no other reason than I thought this was an awesome opportunity to get some really beautiful fashion photos and write them off as a business expense. The whole thing was more a vanity project for me than a brilliant marketing strategy. The firm took the day off, and we spent it getting primped and drinking while we took the shots. And they were beautiful and extremely fashiony, as if shot for *Vanity Fair*. The pictures went out in various law magazines and on our website.

I was not prepared for the reaction. I received numerous calls from lawyers who said we love the photos, we hate the photos, we are confused about the photos not being suitably "lawyerlike." Articles were even written on the subject, saying that we looked more like a made-for-TV law firm than a real one. Obviously, we'd hit a nerve. The more I pushed people to explain to me what they found so unusual about the photographs, the more the rather mundane truth emerged. The fact was that people were shocked that in our official firm portrait I was wearing a dress *that showed my arms*. In other words, I was not wearing a blazer. I understand that the idea that I have arms is shocking, but I didn't think revealing them would be viewed as unlawyerly. In fact, the whole picture apparently did not show lawyers who were stressed, looking serious enough, or hold-ing briefcases. I found it funny, and surprising, that the legal profession thought that a member of the public looking for a lawyer to hire really cared whether we were carrying a briefcase or had our arms folded in a photograph.

For the next photo shoot, I wore a black jacket to cover my arms—but with punky hair and thick black eyeliner. I told the photographer to make it look as though I had just stepped out of a club. And for the next holiday season, we sent out a card with a photo of the firm showing some of us with arms crossed, others holding briefcases, all looking profoundly uncomfortable and very serious, with an incongruous explo-sion of fire behind us. When you opened the card, music played, a song from the Heavy with the refrain "How you like me now?" Some people got it, most did not.

None of this was an attempt at a revolt or meant to buck the system of justice that I believe in. It was, however, an asser-tion that following the party line, looking like what everyone expected, behaving in the way that was least offensive or most innocuous, just was not in my core. It is not who I am and it is not what our firm is about. That is the "brand." People do not hire lawyers because in a photo they are holding a briefcase. Potential clients are far more sophisticated and knowledgeable than our profession gives them credit for. Any casual reading on successful brands tells you that brands that are readily identifi-able and successful do not seek to appeal to everyone. The legal profession has not picked up on this fact. They want to be liked by every potential client, although few members of the public would think likeability is a winning strategy for a law firm.

I would later be told that this one photo helped change the way that law firms were prepared to advertise, although I can't say that for sure. I was not interested in sending any message at all.

What it comes down to is, I just wanted to do what I wanted to do. Sort of a punk ethic. Being closer to who I am in a professional context has always been at the core of our firm. I knew certain things about what I wanted. I wanted to have partners who were unafraid, who were prepared to have confidence in my sometimes out-of-the-box ideas, and who shared a less than conventional vision of what we could be. And above all, I wanted to work in a firm that I enjoyed coming in to every day. That was the one rule that has remained inviolable all these years. And it is with that in mind that I hired who I hired to fill those empty offices.

I started receiving calls from a Bay Street firm about one of their associates, Danielle Robitaille. I was told that although she'd been offered a position in the civil litigation department, her heart was in criminal law and could I consider hiring her as much as it pained them to let her go. I agreed to meet. She happened to be working at the firm where my brother was an associate and he called me with a dire warning. He told me he didn't think Danielle would be a good fit for me.

"Why?" I asked.

"Because she's too happy. It'll annoy you."

"Exactly how happy is too happy?" I asked.

"Labrador retriever puppy happy."

Pete knows me. His warning was serious because too much happiness interferes with my daily not happy disposition. I agreed to meet her anyway.

If you encounter Danielle and you do not instantly like her, there must be something wrong with you. It was hard to resist her infectious upbeat personality or her willingness to work as hard as it takes. I wasn't looking to hire another lawyer, but after spending a week fending off calls from senior partners at her firm telling me I must hire her, I relented. That was well over a decade ago, and we are now law partners and, more importantly, good friends. Danielle is an extraordinary lawyer whose deliberateness in a courtroom is strategic. Don't let the smile fool you.

I quickly learned that an initial interview rarely gives you the true measure of a person. Some people make good first impressions and others do not. That doesn't tell you what type of lawyer or colleague they will be. So most of my hiring decisions in those early days, the very growth of the firm, turned only on gut feeling.

The next cluster of calls I received were entreaties to meet a brilliant young lawyer, a law school gold medallist who had just finished clerking for Chief Justice Beverley McLachlin. The person who walked into my office, Matthew Gourlay, was dishevelled, his tie askew, wiping sweat off his brow with a handkerchief. He barely said a word throughout the interview. I asked him why he had decided to meet with me since mine was a new firm with an uncertain future. The most he could muster was that he had heard good things. I told him there was no position available but that I had also heard good things about him. I suggested that he try some other firms for a job and think it over. It was a brief, wholly uncomfortable meeting.

One week later, Matt called me. When I answered, he said, "Okay."

"Okay what?" I said.

"Okay, I'll take the job."

And there it was. I hired him even though, again, I didn't know whether I had enough work to keep a new lawyer busy. He too is now one of my partners. He is nothing short of encyclopedic in his knowledge of virtually everything, especially the law. A few months into his position, he disclosed that he had fallen for another Supreme Court of Canada clerk, also a gold medallist, who was prepared to move to Toronto but had no job. I told him I would hire her. And so Christine Mainville, brilliant and probably the most defence-oriented of the lot of us, joined our firm. She is our collective conscience whenever any of our cynicism creeps in. There is no client she has met that doesn't warrant empathy.

I still have not seen the résumés of Danielle, Matt, or Christine, although I keep threatening that one day I will ask for them. These were people that struck me as simply too good not to work with.

For years, the firm was Henein and Associates. I had spoken to Eddie often about growing a firm and having a true partner, as opposed to associates. Although Eddie had partners, including me, they were partners in name only. I wanted a true partner, someone who was senior and wanted to create something, because at some point it occurred to me that in order to keep the people I worked with, I had to develop a firm that would have a lifespan beyond my own career.

Scott Hutchison and I have known each other our entire careers. He was a couple of years ahead of me at law school and he was part of what I like to call the brat pack at the appellate Crown Attorney's office. These were an incredibly smart core group of Crown Attorneys, many of whom are now judges, who did all of the significant appellate cases and were frequently before the Supreme Court of Canada. At the time, the appellate bar was relatively small. There were a few of us on the defence side and a few on the Crown side, and Scott and I litigated against each other repeatedly, usually to the death. The two of us enjoyed it as sport, as I did with most of my friends at the appellate office. The night before an appeal was to be argued, it would not be unusual to get together to do a nonpartisan breakdown of the case, fight in court, then go for a drink afterwards for a further debrief. In that circle of advocates, no legal fight was ever personal; it was collegial but equally hard fought.

This core group of people gradually began to disperse from the Crown's office. Unfortunately, the government is not great at recognizing and promoting talented lawyers. Everyone is treated the same, so it is not surprising that the stars eventually look elsewhere—whether it is to become judges or to make the leap to the private bar. After Scott had been at the Crown's appellate office for over a decade, he was recruited into a civil litigation firm. He and I continued to litigate against each other in a regulatory context, where he would represent professional colleges and I would represent the professional. And then one day, we were asked to do a case together, on a pro bono basis, in relation to a right to get adequate legal aid funding for criminal cases. Scott and I were tasked to lead the Toronto portion of the application. After two decades, we finally had the opportunity to litigate on the same side rather than opposite each other, and while the latter had always been fun, we discovered that the former was far better. So I asked him if he would consider taking the risk of leaving a secure, high-paying job to join me as a partner with no guarantees and no plans for how or what we would grow into. I told him that asking him to be my partner wasn't part of a grand business strategy but simply because the idea of litigating together for the next two decades was too much fun to pass up. He agreed, and so Henein Hutchison LLP was born.

Our firm of four doubled, then tripled, and then quadrupled. We found people who we wanted to work with, who would mesh with our view of how to be effective lawyers, committed to litigation, and we grew from there. Obviously a firm this size has a different feel, but along the way, every single fundamental decision was made based on a gut check. Our firm continues to grow and develop beyond anything I planned or imagined when I left Eddie's with two boxes. I enjoy going to work. I enjoy working with my colleagues, and there is no other group that I would rather go into a tough fight with than the quirky, very smart people I work with. If you do not enjoy where you have to spend the majority of your life, if you do not believe in the intellect and commitment of your colleagues and they in you, then no amount of business planning, lunching, branding, or marketing will give you the heart you need to keep going.

The day it stops being fun, the day I stop wanting to walk into that office, is the day that I will quit.

A few years ago, I invited my family to attend an event of sixteen hundred lawyers that I was speaking at. At the end of my speech, I looked out into the crowd and could not miss my father, there, watching in disbelief. And it was as though we were on the phone again, all those years ago when I was starting out on my own. I looked at him and said, "Dad, it's okay now, I think *they* know I'm out here."

10

SORRY, NOT SORRY

I AM OFTEN ASKED WHY I became a criminal defence lawyer. Not in a "that is really interesting" way but as if to say, "Why on earth would you choose something so *unseemly*?" It's as if I should be sorry for my choice of profession and its lack of gentility, and for doing the job that men have monopolized for years.

A recent spate of public notoriety as a result of some high-profile cases I've taken has resulted in apparent impropriety on my part. None of it deliberate, I assure you. I've become used to being described as "controversial" or "polarizing," although I admit that for a time I couldn't figure out why. Given that most people do not know my views on a wide range of issues or my political predispositions, it's perplexing to be categorized as inherently divisive. The fact is, I am neither polarizing nor controversial; what is, is my choice of profession.

Nonetheless, I now commonly receive a sheepish call before a scheduled lecture to alert me that an objection has been registered by some group or other to my speaking, most commonly to university students on campus. Usually, these objections are voiced before anyone even knows exactly what subject I am going to talk about. I am not a provocateur by nature, nor am I a fan of those who seek to provoke for no reason other than the notoriety that accompanies it. The shock provocateur sells and, no question, provides a bit of catharsis to those who have some delusion that they are under imminent siege from the "other" but it is not my game.

Ideologies and siege mentality aside, however, I have developed a perverse tolerance for the provocateurs among us, if for no other reason than that they seem to be the only ones these days prepared to offer themselves up to be challenged. These shock-talkers willingly expose themselves, literally begging us to take a shot at them, so I figure the least we can do is jump at the chance and take the shot to challenge their silly ideas. Silencing them does not eradicate their message. Sadly, polite society rarely takes them up on the offer, since taking offence is easier than direct ideological engagement through dialogue. When did we all become so thin-skinned?

Anyway, I did not expect to find myself in a category of controversials. I don't like them much, to be honest. I naively thought I could criss-cross the country talking about the justice system with those who wanted to know how it works, its purpose, where we fail, where we succeed. I am a lawyer, after all, and this is my field of expertise, and no matter how sensitive or closed off you are to other points of view, I would have thought open discussions about the law are hardly something to cause the vapours, at least not to the extent where I get banned from speaking. But "provocative" and "controversial" is where I have involuntarily found myself.

The very thought of me and my choice of profession seemingly causes a stir in the now rarefied academic enclaves where challenging thought has been replaced by a sensitive genteelness more appropriate to a Victorian parlour, and where the mere thought of an unpleasant comment can bring on nervous shock. One institution, which will go unnamed, went so far as to make counsellors available in the lecture hall where I was speaking and preceded my introduction with the requisite trigger warnings. The topic of my speech? Democratic institutions and the justice system, a subject that should not trigger a single rational, or even irrational, soul. Before one speech titled "Women and Leadership," the organizer let me know that there were strong objections to the event from certain quarters. I asked her if there was something objectionable about discussing women in leadership roles. "No," she said, "it's just you," which is sort of a problem since I come along with any speech I am invited to give. Invariably, the organizer whose job it is to invite me to the event bends over backwards trying to explain to the audience why I was invited at all, usually excusing her- or himself by disavowing my clients or otherwise trying to somehow soften the blow, as if to say, *Don't be offended by her, she doesn't really mean it.* But I do. I *mean* to be a criminal defence lawyer. This is no accident.

It is frustrating to be the target of derision. Usually, I just smile and proceed with my speech as planned, as though I wasn't insulted just moments before, but I confess that my impatience is getting the better of me these days. I've been sorely tempted to stand up and tell the audience that I'm out of there. It would be a fun bit of drama. But then I remind myself that this is nothing more than my own petulance and it will result in a lost opportunity to encourage dialogue. Effective discourse takes self-control, inside the courtroom and out. Inside I can manage. It's on the outside that takes work these days.

We have to give some thought as to why the public finds criminal defence lawyers, particularly female ones, so provocative. Despite moments of crisis in which criminal defence lawyers have been viewed as necessary and valued fighters for the unpopular or marginalized, most of the time we are at the receiving end of a great deal of criticism. This is because most people don't like lawyers to begin with. And while we criminal lawyers have defended the likes of Émile Zola, the Chicago Seven, Robert Mapplethorpe, Flaubert, and Voltaire, we have also defended the Manson family, Ernst Zündel, Timothy McVeigh, and Harvey Weinstein.

What's unpalatable to members of the public is that we defend both people whom the public think are virtuous and those whom they think are not. Defence lawyers draw no distinction in the professional service we provide to each group. In deciding who to represent, the lawyer's refusal to distinguish between the morally righteous and the blameworthy polarizes, is provocative, and leads to an assumption that what is truly at play is either the lawyer's moral ambiguity or, worse still, their amorality.

But those of us in the profession, and the profession itself, are neither amoral nor morally ambiguous; in fact, the line is very clear to us. In exercising my professional obligations as a defence lawyer, I cannot allow myself to make such distinctions. That we keep some form of a morality score card is a fundamental misconception of our role. If our job was to determine the guilt or innocence of our own clients, to render moral judgment and act as judge and jury, the role of judges and prosecutors would become redundant. The ethics of a criminal defence lawyer requires zealous advocacy on behalf of a client. It does not allow for the lawyer to make moral judgments, and neither does it allow for less vigorous advocacy depending on our view of the client or their conduct. The right to a lawyer, the right to a defence, cannot be reserved for only those who win public approval or popularity contests. To accord a defence to only those deemed worthy obviously sets a dangerous precedent, not least because history has taught us that mob rule is fickle and usually victimizes the weak, the unpopular, the marginalized. I have no confidence in those who think they can divine who in society should be entitled to a vigorous defence and who should not. A differential dispensation of justice is corrupt and can only lead to injustice and miscarriages of justice.

There are two reasons why this lesson does not seep into our collective conscience. First, we either don't know our history or simply don't learn from it. Second, we are invariably subjective in our assessment of most things. The perceived success or failure of the criminal justice system depends on where you are sitting at any particular time, whether you won or lost or whether the judge decided the way you thought the case should go. But the creation and application of good law requires the discipline of objectivity no matter what side of it you're on. The flaws in the legal system that a victim would identify are different from those that a wrongfully accused person would focus on. Both are valuable perspectives to consider, but neither is determinative.

Competing interests and objectives make for the painful calibration of the justice system. The system is imperfect, and at some point, some party will be unsatisfied with where the needle has come to rest. As with most things, you cannot have it all. No one emerges from the criminal justice process celebrating how great the experience has been. This is why asking how we can make the criminal process less painful or less intimidating is a wrongheaded question. The evaluation of the justice system, particularly the criminal justice system, has to be anchored in something other than how good it makes one feel: it has to be based on our core democratic and constitutional values, and can't be altered by the whims of a fickle government or its constituents to make some happy. Any metric requires us to ask the right questions: is the system fair, is everyone able to be heard, does it provide for the best circumstances to allow for adjudication, and does it facilitate the discovery of truth?

Here are the questions I get asked most often as a criminal defence lawyer: How can you defend someone you know is guilty? How can you defend someone charged with a heinous crime? How can you, as a woman, defend a man charged with sexual assault? How can you, as a parent, defend someone charged with abusing a child? The list of moral dilemmas that the public assumes present me with a personal struggle as a defence lawyer is endless. The truth is, I do not consider myself to be ethically challenged or morally compromised by my choice of profession. Not one bit—just as a doctor is not ethically challenged when performing surgery on a morally dubious patient or any person the public does not think is worth saving. We give medical treatment to all, even if you have a criminal record. And we don't assume doctors are morally bankrupt for doing so. My clients do not hire me for my personal assessment of their moral character. And the law, my professional obligations, demand that I leave those personal judgments out of my work, just as doctors take the Hippocratic oath. Judging my clients is the very antithesis of my professional obligation.

Notable academics have wrestled with these very same questions. "Can a good lawyer be a good person?" was the first line of a seminal paper by Harvard professor Charles Fried in 1976. Numerous academics have spilled a sea of ink on this dilemma, so let me give you the answer plain and simple: Yes, they can. And are.

Most people's interaction with the criminal justice system is peripheral—a traffic ticket at most. When what's at stake is a small fine, the gamesmanship of it can easily be the stuff of water cooler talk. But the criminal process is not a game. Not a single accused person views it this way when their freedom is at stake. The desperate need for certainty that life will go back to normal becomes overwhelming, and it is an assurance that lawyers cannot provide. The only comfort that we can offer is the promise that we will hear the client out, do our best, and present the strongest case possible. Unless you find yourself sitting in my office, with the full machinery of the government bearing down on you, fighting for your freedom and everything you hold dear, and realizing that bad things, including accusations, can happen to basically decent people, you probably observe the justice system from a comfortable distance.

Not many get a front-row seat, but when they do, their perspective changes dramatically. The looking glass reveals a scary, often incomprehensible, world. Accused people and victims of crime often feel completely lost when navigating the process, and often fail to understand what the very limited function of the criminal justice system really is—not retribution, not vindication, not closure. Those are buzzwords that have nothing to do with the real experience of a criminal court. And it is wrong to go looking to a courtroom for that sort of comfort. The criminal process has only one function, and that is to determine whether the state has proved the case against an individual beyond a reasonable doubt such that the deprivation of liberty is warranted. No more and no less. Social policy is not formed in a criminal trial. In fact, by the time we find ourselves at the courtroom door, the bad thing, the crime, has already occurred. We as a society have already failed. The criminal trial is not a retroactive fix for our social failures.

Every single client of mine has been shell-shocked by the criminal process. Virtually all of them began by asking the same questions: Is this all it takes to charge a person? Can anyone just go to the police and make an accusation? Pretty much, yes. In its crudest form, that is exactly how it works.

I've given up trying to explain to those I represent the precise role of the police and the Crown. It gives them little comfort. I've also given up explaining that "she said" or "he said" is actually evidence that the court can properly rely on. People's words are evidence, and not everything is *CSI* and forensics. If that was the standard, very few cases would go to court. In many instances, all it takes to set things in motion is for a person to walk into a police station and make a statement to an officer.

The threshold for the police to criminally charge someone is relatively low, and investigative acumen is a wide variable. To be criminally charged, there is no requirement of objective or extrinsic evidence. In most jurisdictions, there is little prosecutorial oversight of the police and their investigative function, although some have initiated a pre-charge screening mechanism. This means that charges cannot be laid unless approved by a prosecutor who has reviewed the evidence. Pre-charge screening is the exception, however. In most jurisdictions, the police have the full and unfettered authority to investigate and lay criminal charges. Once a prosecutor and an objective arbiter, such as a judge or jury, is involved, the accused has the opportunity to present a defence. But that provides little solace to those who find themselves on the other side of the law. At the preliminary stages, the resounding feeling of most of the accused is one of helplessness and loss of control. This is doubled if your freedom has been taken away while you await trial, a fate that is common, particularly for those who are poor or mentally ill. In both Canada and the United States, an unconscionable number of individuals are held in jail, in limbo, presumed innocent, awaiting their day in court.

Stunned by the immediacy with which life as they know it is taken away—from jobs to savings to access to their children to friends—and by how powerless they really are when caught up in the machinery of the state, I've never had a client sit in my office and clap their hands together as they celebrate all the constitutional rights they've suddenly inherited as an accused.

These rights are not reserved just for an accused. It is when someone is charged with a crime and becomes an accused, however, that they are activated. Every citizen has the same rights. The Constitution protects all of us. If the police break down your door and find nothing, that is usually the end of the matter. You may be upset about the constitutional breach, but you will not, unless you choose to sue the police, have any occasion to assert your right against unreasonable search and seizure. Unchecked, the police can, and do, use their power disproportionately. The same is true of the state when it seeks to criminalize speech, or abortion, or a million other things we take for granted. The institutional check often comes about in the context of a criminal trial. That is when the litigation of these constitutional rights occurs. So if the police knock down your door and find drugs, and as a result you are criminally charged, you will assert that right to be secure against unreasonable searches.

Here is the thing to remember: the parameters of what the police and the state can and cannot do, where they can tread upon your privacy and where they cannot, is often litigated and defined in the context of criminal cases. Police and state limits are tested and challenged in that criminal courtroom courtesy of someone most members of the public think very little of—the accused. But each and every citizen benefits from and has the protection of these constitutional constraints on state power. The accused do not have "all the rights." We all have them, all the time. The difference is that the accused may be required to assert them.

I am not interested in mounting a defence of criminal lawyers or being an apologist for my profession. It is the attack on the choice of this profession, the utter disregard for what the role of a defence lawyer is, that is problematic. We need, collectively, to try to understand, and critically think about, the role of the justice system as a whole when the very function of a key component in that system is so widely misunderstood and under fire. What this requires is discipline in our assessment of the system so that it extends beyond a specific case or type of offence to the entirety of the judicial construct and why it is valuable in protecting our most essential values.

For the moment, let's focus on the role of the lawyer. Anyone who enters the field of criminal law is acutely aware of the importance of their role in the judicial, and indeed social, fabric that we value. That is why people become criminal defence lawyers—because they believe in democratic values, the protection of the minority, and the need to challenge institutional power.

There is a reflexive inclination to conflate a lawyer with their client. Confusing me with my client is at the heart of the question *How can you do what you do?* This is the kind of thinking that comes from viewing the issue in isolation, disconnected from the justice system as a whole. But viewed in context, grounded by a regard for our foundational democratic aspirations, the imperative of the criminal lawyer's role should be self-evident.

There is an old adage that a lawyer defends the client and not the crime. I have never met a criminal lawyer who is pro-crime or, indeed, indifferent to crime. That is just not a normal human predisposition. We all want to be safe, criminal lawyers included. Nobody goes to law school with the goal of making society less safe. To think so is perverse. After some of the back-lash I have faced over the years—in the media, in cancelled speaking engagements, in the elevator, walking in the hospital to visit my mom, wherever—it's important to say this: I have defended people charged with murder. That does not mean that I am a proponent, supporter, or facilitator of murder. I have acted for people charged with all sorts of crimes. That does not mean that I am a proponent, supporter, or facilitator of those crimes, or of any crime. And it's worth remembering that the work of a criminal lawyer also routinely involves acting for *victims* of crime, those that want and need guidance through the legal system or just don't know how to approach the police or make a complaint. That too is the job of a criminal lawyer.

Criminal lawyers have to be resolute—immovable—in their belief in the presumption of innocence *for everyone* and the need for the state to prove its case beyond a reasonable doubt *for everyone*. It is the "for everyone" part that the public views with opprobrium, as though there is a reliable barometer that can accurately determine who should be accorded the full protection of the law and who should not. History tells us this is not so—it is impossible to calibrate a fair legal system that accords rights differentially based on who the person is, what the crime is or any other arbitrary yardstick. It is precisely the "for everyone" part that makes our justice system just and, at the same time, sometimes difficult to swallow. And that makes the work of a defence lawyer particularly confounding.

In my experience, being a female defence lawyer is par-ticularly polarizing. But then again, being a female anything is. I have come to accept this as just another occupational hazard, of which there are many. Of course, this certainly wasn't part of the equation when I chose my profession. Those before me, almost all men, have been doing the exact same job I've been doing for years, so I figured it would hardly be disruptive if I gave it a shot. But for many people, men and women both, the job seems uniquely unpalatable and unseemly, even traitorous to our sex, when performed by a female. Women defence lawyers may be an anomalous subcategory of a certain species, and we may be few and far between, but traitorous to our sex we are not.

Neither public disapproval nor the fact that female defence lawyers are unicorns has dampened my love for this profession. So why did I choose it? I have been passionate about criminal law for as long as I can remember. There is no easy explanation for this love affair. I didn't have a big personal crisis. I didn't have lawyers in my family to look up to. Part of the real draw for me wanting to become a criminal lawyer was that the profession is built for underdogs and outsiders. The job, when done properly, doesn't allow me to toe the party line. In a legal context, criminal law is one of the places where the status quo is routinely disrupted, or at least challenged. In Canada, think of the challenges to the criminalization of abortion, the legalization of marijuana, the legalization of prostitution, or the right to die. All these cases involved sometimes repeated challenges to the status quo. And all of them were challenges to criminal laws.

My work invariably brings me into conflict with the state, whether it be police officers, prosecutors, or judges. It's not personal or acrimonious. I'm in conflict because I'm required to take up the defence and sometimes the cause of the unpopular. And I need to be resolute in it. I must advance my client's case in the face of many others whose job it is to convict. A criminal lawyer, in many respects, stands on the other side of all of those actors and has the obligation to disrupt the status quo, to challenge the state or the police, to make the prosecutor prove their case. You often do this swimming upstream against the tide of public opinion.

It is important to keep in mind that the role of the lawyer arose as a response to historic abuses of power by the state, such as the Star Chamber. The core theory in its most rudimentary form is that through an adversarial model, an impartial arbiter— the judge—will be able to deliver justice. The difficulty I think we run into with criticisms of the adversarial system is our understanding and expectation of what justice means. Normative justice is elusive. Truth-seeking, while certainly a core component of justice, is constrained by the inherently historical nature of a criminal trial. It is only as accurate or truthful as history can be. This is because a criminal trial is not a real-time scientific experiment. It requires the recreation, largely through verbal testimony, of a historical event. The recreation of a past event, which must also take into account motivations and intentions, will never yield precise or even consistent results. Perceptions of a past event are vastly personal and informed by all sorts of personal bias. The very nature of the exercise, the recreation of a historical event, makes it imprecise and susceptible to error. It also makes the attainment of objective truth a difficult though worthy goal.

The rules of evidence are certainly designed to facilitate truth-seeking, but many other rules are not. For example, the exclusion of potentially reliable evidence, such as a confession, because of a constitutional breach is grounded in another component of justice in the adversarial system—the notion of fairness. The English philosopher Jeremy Bentham, for example, argued that torture was an effective evidence-gathering mechanism. Yet nowadays, waterboarding and other forms of torture are anathema to civil society and not a price we should be willing to pay to get the truth. The tension sometimes inherent between truth-seeking and fairness make the precise mix of the rules and laws that define the justice system complex.

But these two principles, truth-seeking and fairness, also have to inform our assessment of whether justice has been done. This means that in some cases, truth-seeking must give way to fairness. We as a society draw a line in the sand to demarcate our tolerance between these two principles, and we must recognize that it is a shifting line. The use of torture as an evidence gathering tool in the wake of 9/11 has been an ongoing debate—what constitutes torture, whether to use it. We should ask what is driving the shift. Is the willingness to suddenly accept torture as a viable evidence-gathering tool when it comes to terrorists driven by xenophobia? Why wasn't it raised with domestic terrorists like the Oklahoma City bomber? These issues are complex. There is no clear answer, and reasonable people may disagree. The point, however, is that we need to examine *when* we are prepared to shift the balance between truth-seeking and fairness in the justice system at any given particular moment and why. Our motives and assumptions need scrutiny.

What justice does *not* mean is that any participant is entitled to a particular outcome. Justice isn't determined by whether you win or lose in court. The concept of justice incorporates far broader issues than that. It means that principles of fairness—limits of state abuses when it comes to the government's investigation of and attempts to deny the liberty of its own citizens—are constrained.

The adversarial system is not without its many flaws. It is difficult, unfriendly, emotionally trying. It is not a place to seek meaningful closure or retribution. And most participants can only hope to leave with a feeling that they've been heard and had their day in court. The success of the system is also premised of course on the theory that the adversaries are evenly matched, both in skill and resources, although in practice this is not always the case. Marginalized, impoverished justice participants are the greatest victims of this inequality. Unfortunately, lobbying for poor people charged with crimes or for more resources for the system as a whole is a tough sell and not where governments want to spend public money.

There are non-adversarial legal systems in which the role of the defence lawyer is quite different. In inquisitorial systems, for example, it is the examining magistrate that takes the lead in questioning, not the lawyers. The lawyers, particularly defence lawyers, have a limited role to play. Underlying this approach is the belief that a defence lawyer's ethical obligation to society is on equal footing with the lawyer's obligation to the client. This stands in stark contrast to our adversarial system, in which the defence lawyer cannot have any divided loyalties. This does not mean it is a free-for-all. A defence lawyer is constrained by the law, by the rules of evidence and by ethical obligations. While the lawyer must operate within these parameters, a defence lawyer's primary obligation is to defend the client to the best of their ability. This does not mean sleight of hand, dishonesty, or the type of deception that you routinely see fictionalized on TV, none of which leads to effective advocacy. It does mean an unwavering commitment to the client, no matter how difficult that may be.

For me, the relationship between lawyer and client is deeply personal. The most fascinating moments about a case are often those that I cannot speak about, meetings and moments that happen with a client that give insight into them or the events. But, as I said at the start, I cannot share my clients' stories. I can understand never wishing to relive that part of one's life, certainly not publicly and certainly not at the hands of one's lawyer. The relationship between lawyer and client is so sacrosanct that the law recognizes a solicitor–client privilege. This means, in rudimentary form, that anything a client tells a lawyer in the context of that relationship and for the purpose of legal advice can never be disclosed by the lawyer. And no court, with very few exceptions, can compel disclosure from a lawyer.

There are two moments in a criminal trial that powerfully exemplify this duty to the client—when a client stands up to be arraigned, and when they stand up to receive the verdict. During both of those moments, the defence lawyer stands up and takes a position right at the client's side. It is more than mere custom. In those moments, as I stand shoulder to shoulder with my client, it is symbolic that I'm the one person who bears the ethical obligation, the moral responsibility, to stand between my client and the state. Those moments are the physical manifestation of our role.

None of this means that I am impervious to or unaware of the dynamics in the courtroom or the feelings of others. As anyone who has spent substantial time in a courtroom knows, it is a place where there is often a great deal of pain and humanity. But we, I, see it all and see everyone who is there. I know how difficult it is, how emotionally wrought, and the suffering that all participants, victims, accused, and their families go through. There are times, many in fact, where I have left the courtroom utterly exhausted, and it usually takes me a while to regain my equilibrium. For the first few weeks after a trial, I am no good to anyone; then I move on to the next case. All of us in the justice system, in addition to the accused and the witnesses and victims, wear this exhaustion. But a defence lawyer is not entitled to share that while doing their job. The defence lawyer must be single-minded and emotionally constrained. It is what the law expects of us.

This is something I had to learn as a young lawyer. I had been involved in a lengthy case with Eddie Greenspan. One of the witnesses who testified was, to me anyway, extremely sympathetic, and it was heartbreaking to hear her story. After court, I expressed to Eddie my empathy for the witness and how difficult I'd found it to listen to her testimony. "That witness," Eddie roared, "is here to make sure our client is convicted. That is the only thing you need to spend your time thinking about." Time and again, this lesson was drummed into me. A lawyer's emotions, their personal views, must be checked. There is little room for them. A defence lawyer's obligation lies in one direction only.

The clients, funnily enough, are perhaps the most surprised by this. Whenever a client asks me, "Do you believe me?" I always give the same answer: "You are asking the wrong question." My job, my ethical obligation, is to act in my client's best interests, and that is why my personal opinions, my views, my feelings have no place in my office or in a courtroom. Except in the rare case, I do not have the right or permission to take a moral stance. If I ever thought I did have a view that I could not set aside, then I would not act for that client. And there is no shame in that, either. There are lawyers who restrict their practice to certain types of cases and refuse to do others. I am not one of them.

I didn't understand any of that when I decided to become a criminal defence lawyer. The work, the subject matter, all of it is who I am at my core. It was the right fit. That was the real draw. And I love a good fight. Maybe it's my Arab disposition. I love the subject matter and commitment to individual rights. I like fighting for the underdog against state power. I love the uphill battle. The work, notwithstanding that it is trying and often emotionally depleting, is the amalgamation of things that work well with my personality and intellectual interests.

I have always been obsessed with criminal law. I quite simply love the law. I read about the law, I've never met a movie or show about the law that I didn't watch (even as I railed against the inaccurate, cartoonish depiction of defence lawyers), and I spend most of my free time talking about the law. And being in a courtroom is where I feel most at home. The minute I have navigated the courthouse and settled in the courtroom, the moment that the clerk announces that court is in session, I am at home.

To those who view what I do as unseemly, or think that it's traitorous, I am proud of the work I do.

In short, sorry, not sorry.

11

TAKE A BREATH

SOME DAYS I CONVINCE MYSELF that the legal system is as unassailable as the Sphinx, solid and immovable. It is false comfort, though, because nothing is ever unassailable. Weathering centuries of desert storms, even the Sphinx was not impervious to losing her nose. She had been a sitting duck for a long time, exposed to anyone who wanted to take a shot. Sure, the Sphinx still sits majestically exactly where she always has, just without a nose; damaged, a little less than what she originally was. Interestingly, in legal writing, the role of the judge is often compared to that of the Sphinx—immutable, untouchable, impervious to any shots taken.

Lately, I've come to believe it's not true. Like the Sphinx, the justice system is equally vulnerable to attack—from politicians, driven by the digital mob—one of our most important democratic foundations is on shakey ground.

Social media is the lens through which we now often assess many things, from news to ourselves, and it is naive to think that the justice system is immune to the digital distortion we all fall victim to. Think of this. Before the advent of social media, what occurred in a courtroom was covered only by experienced, knowledgeable court reporters. In addition, there was a built-in cooling-off period because the public needed to wait until that evening or the next day to learn about what had occurred in a given trial. The expectation was that the goings-on of a courtroom would be reported through the neutral lens of a professional journalist who understood the contours of what was happening. In my experience, many people think they have a good grasp of what is occurring in a courtroom, and why; but the fact is, they don't. Watching every season of *Law & Order* does not make you an expert. The legal system can be like a foreign language, and it takes a lot of work and knowledge to translate it. This is not to say that all court reporting is good or even wholly accurate, but it's pretty consistent, and most of the people who do it are pros who have been around the courtroom block.

But now, with the speed and scope of social media, anyone, anywhere, can comment on what is happening in a trial without stepping foot in the courtroom, and these opinions can be consumed by millions of people within minutes. And all in 140 characters of a tweet whose power far exceeds its constitution or composition. Unfiltered and uncurated, the public is left to discern what is and is not true. Having lived with social media for several years now, we know that it is easy to incite the mob. Jon Ronson, in his book *So You've Been Publicly Shamed*, gives numerous examples of ordinary people who have been outed on social media and have had their careers, if not their lives, destroyed because the digital mob, incited to outrage, has demanded their heads on a platter. In the old days, wading into a public shaming required a person to actually step outside of their home and engage with the mob. Now, it can be done from the convenience of one's couch, in complete anonymity. You don't even have to stand up to throw stones.

The democratization of communication through social media has value, bringing to the fore stories and views that historically have no platform and no audience. But it is important to filter our reliance on social media by remembering that it is unrestricted and posting a blog does not require a single qualification. Not all commentary is created equally or, more accurately, created by people who are equally qualified to make it. This brave new electronic global village cannot be rewound. I am not advocating that it should be. It is not reasonable or practical to think that social-media commentary can be meaningfully censored or that we can trust Facebook, Google, or Twitter to do that filtering. They are corporations that owe us and our democracy nothing. But we do still have control over one thing—our reactions. We do not have to simply agree with other people's conclusions. We still have independent will, even in the digital age. We do not have to be persuaded by or believe everything we read. And surely our reaction, mob-like in its intensity and quickness, should be held in check.

The internet lacks integrity. It doesn't have a truthfulness or accuracy meter. In fact, as numerous writers have identified, the people that hold the key to information that is disseminated to us from Facebook to Google do not filter for truthfulness or accuracy. The disseminators can't be trusted to be knowledgeable, much less give us the whole truth. So it falls upon us, the users, to attempt to discern what is and is not real, and what is and is not worth reacting to.

Here's my worry. Sorting the fake news from the real news is hard enough, but add to that the challenge of sourcing informed, reasoned, non-inflammatory commentary and it is no wonder that the public is frequently and quickly inflamed about the justice system. If QAnon can convince thousands of people that the Democrats are a pedophilic secret society, why would we think that the justice system is immune from digital distortion?

I'm still an optimist. I think that if the public is provided with good old-fashioned information, they will be able to engage in a meaningful debate and ask the right questions. An informed public is the antidote to a mob, seduced as it is by the speed of the technology at hand, its own ignorance of facts and history, and its need to do something, anything, in the name of "justice."

Let's face it, there have always been those among us who know how the justice system works and those who don't. The problem I have with the internet is that it empowers and amplifies those who don't, often making them believe they are in the know. So maybe it is time for some basics—Justice 101—not to convince you of anything but just to add to your informational arsenal so that the next time you read a tweet about a court case, you might have some questions of your own that you want answered.

Let's start by admitting the obvious: the justice system is built on a shaky foundation. We want judges to be sphinx-like. We expect them to check their personal views at the courthouse doors and focus only on the admissible evidence introduced in court. The problem is that it's hard to aspire to pure objectivity when the system is built on the backs of humans. The Anglo-American justice system strives to achieve the ideal of the sphinx-like judge by tinkering with the rules of evidence. We do this to try to insulate the decider from distractions that, while not wholly irrelevant, would carry a disproportionate weight of the burden of proof. We do everything we can to prevent the decision-making in a trial from being improperly subjective.

In other words, there are times that evidence, while admittedly relevant, is so peripheral, distracting, or inflammatory that it must be taken out of the adjudicative process. In order to preserve the judge or jury's ability to make an objective finding, we restrict the evidence to that which will help determine the essential question before the court: guilt or innocence. That is, after all, the only issue in a criminal court. Rules of evidence are designed to force disciplined thinking and, hopefully, equally disciplined decision-making.

The media and politicians often mischaracterize the law as obstructing truth-seeking. This kind of misinformation could not be more destructive. The legal system is not a game, and the rules of a trial are not designed to frustrate the process or disproportionately help one side over the other. They are designed to imbue a human process with as much objectivity as possible.

Removing the built-in prejudices of a human process is a tall order. We often hear complaints about evidence being "kept" from the jury, as though this were done for some nefarious purpose. It is a common refrain, but it is simply not true. Evidence is not kept from the decider to undermine the truth-seeking function. Quite the opposite, in fact.

Let me illustrate with a concrete example of how this works in a criminal trial. Most people would say the fact that an accused has a criminal history is a relevant piece of information. This is because, as a matter of human experience, we know that people often act in the way they have acted previously. Past conduct is a common-sense predictor of future behaviour. The same is true of criminal behaviour. So it is not unreasonable to assume that if someone has committed a crime in the past, they are more likely to have subsequently committed a similar crime they are now being accused of.

But we also know that this is not always the case. This gut reaction is, in fact, often inaccurate. Past behaviour doesn't automatically mean the person committed the crime they are being accused of. The relevance of past behaviour as a predictor of future behaviour depends on a lot of things, such as the person and the nature and circumstances of the crime. The assumption that people necessarily act in conformity with the way they have acted before, which we know is not always true, can lead to miscarriages of justice and sloppy police work. If criminal history was presumptively viewed as a significant indicator of guilt, police would simply round up the usual suspects every time a crime was committed. We know that this is an ineffective method of policing that leads to highly discriminatory practices. We also know that judges and juries may be inclined to believe that because someone committed a crime in the past, there is no need to look closely at the evidence in relation to the crime they are being tried for. They get lazy because of this human inclination to jump to conclusions.

So do we exclude all criminal history? Sometimes it is a helpful piece of information, other times it is not. The answer is not straightforward. Recognizing the complexity of the problem, the law attempts to neutralize the prejudice that can result from allowing a decider to know of an accused's criminal record. As a general rule, criminal records are inadmissible against an accused, but as with everything in the law, nothing is a straight line. There are significant exceptions. For example, where the previous crime is so similar to the current crime, that it would be unlikely that two different people committed them, criminal history may be admitted. A criminal history can also be admitted if it reveals a marker, or signature way, of committing a crime and therefore helps the decider consider the question of the identity of the perpetrator. Prior criminal history is not hidden from a jury. It is admitted if it assists in the adjudication of a case and excluded if it will distract or lead to error because it will be given too much importance. Courts look at the probative value of evidence and its potential prejudicial effect. Even when a criminal record is admitted, the law requires that its use be strictly focused on the issue at hand. The court cannot use it to conclude that because the accused has done something bad before, they must have done the bad thing that they are now charged with.

There are hundreds of similar examples of how the law attempts to strike a difficult balance and focus the decider's task on what is relevant to the specific case before them. Striking the correct balance depends on the nature of the defence, the nature of the facts at issue in a case, and whether the evidence is probative of any of those facts.

If none of this sounds inflammatory, that is because it isn't. The law is a meticulous, tedious, painstaking grind. The law creates general rules and then has to apply them to widely disparate fact patterns, because there is no end to the types of crimes and the ways in which they can be committed. Similarly, there is no standard trial. The facts and issues differ with each and every case. Although the approach is methodical, this does not mean that we all agree. The Crown and defence can argue opposite sides of the very same piece of evidence. And different judges, because the process is human, can come to the opposite conclusion entirely. That doesn't make the system inherently corrupt or flawed. It makes it what it is: a human process that can lead to different views and results.

I am not saying this to give you a lesson on evidence, but to make clear that the law is complex, and how we decide cases is not simply determined by who we think we believe. Nor is it determined by political views or gut feelings. Deciding a case requires analysis, careful thought, and, most importantly, discipline in not jumping to conclusions—all of which is antithetical to the way people act on the internet. By the time the judge or jury have sifted through all the evidence, they should be looking at only the evidence that matters to the particular case. Public sentiment or personal reputation should have no part in that analysis.

People understand this on an intuitive level, but when we disagree with the result of a criminal trial or stumble on a tweet decrying that the judge excluded evidence, it is easy to view the justice system as disconnected from our social needs or desires. I recognize that the justice system sometimes does feel and is out of step with society. But even in those moments, we shouldn't be reflexive and try to change it in a way that we as a society will come to regret.

As I've said, the justice system is not perfect. It reflects our own failings. Humans adjudicate, litigate, testify, and make the laws. Every single part of it bears the imprint of our flawed humanity. There are those who have tried to sanitize it, to make the whole adjudicative process more scientific and less susceptible to the whims of our humanity, but they have failed. A trial is not a mathematical formula; nor is it a science experiment that can be replicated time and again. We will get different results in different courtrooms with different people.

We also need to remember that while our human frailties are the source of some of the greatest failings of the justice system, the ability to respond humanely is also one of its greatest strengths. At least that is my experience. The ability of the justice system to make unpopular decisions in the face of external, even political, forces, and to protect minority and disenfranchised members of the community, or show compassion in sentencing—all those attributes stem from its very humanity.

I am no Pollyanna. Having spent over a quarter of a century in this business, I know that it stumbles. But I also know that it is the best we've got. When we hear complaints that the justice system has failed, the dissatisfaction stems from the fact that our expectations are misaligned with what the courtroom, particularly a criminal court, is equipped to do. The one thing a criminal court is not designed to do is to wrestle with our broader social issues.

The solutions to those fundamental problems begin well before we ever set foot in a courtroom. For example, you can take away rights in a court, and go straight to sentencing each and every time, but you will have very little impact on gun crimes. Because the reason for gun crimes, the easy accessibility of guns, remains the essential problem. No amount of courtroom action—from denying bail to stiff sentencing—will ever solve that problem. The court is quite simply not equipped to address access to guns. A get-tough-on-drugs policy did not do one single thing to stem the tide of drug use in the United States or Canada. It did, however, create an epidemic of mass incarceration and racialize the prison population even more. The drug problem remains because drug addiction will never be solved in a courtroom. Some countries recognize this limitation and have begun to look beyond courts for real solutions treating drug crimes as addictions and not moral failures. Social policy and criminal courtrooms are not good bedfellows.

Understanding this reality—that social problems are rarely created or solved inside a courthouse—we should ask why the "soft on crime" criticism is a go-to move for politicians of all stripes. Why do most crime bills that add offences, increase sentences, or establish mandatory minimum sentences generally go unopposed regardless of political stripes?

The answer is simple. Tough-on-crime agendas are a winning political play. The demonization of others always is, especially when the target is the marginalized and racialized among us. In the United States, where a conviction precludes many people from the right to vote, you can easily understand why elected officials do not view individuals embroiled in the criminal system as an important demographic.

Furthermore, politicians often use the criminal justice system to advance their own agendas. Espousing the language of fear—usually through the demonization of the accused, the lawyer or the judge—is a deliberate mechanism that creates a rift between the public and the justice system so that, rather than the institution being viewed as a protector of the public, it is viewed with suspicion, and portrayed as unconnected to the plight of the common person. The politician, rather than the justice system, is presented as the true protector of the people, and in those times, "The system is broken" becomes a familiar refrain.

Why else do you think politicians so quickly latch on to this language, claiming that crime is at an all-time high or that we are unsafe on our own streets, even when the statistics prove that the opposite is true? It is a ploy, and as far as ploys go, it's a pretty effective one. A judge who releases a person on bail or doesn't hand out the stiffest possible sentence can be portrayed as insensitive to public safety compared with the politician who calls for stiffer sentences.

It always fascinates me how get-tough-on-crime policies receive bipartisan support. I have yet to see any political party show the integrity and internal fortitude to be honest when they approach criminal justice reform. That is because their response is rarely evidence-based. Just look at the history of the war on drugs. While the mantle was picked by President Ronald Reagan, it was in fact Richard Nixon who first declared a war on drugs, and by extension drug dealers and users. At a press conference in 1971, Nixon identified drug abuse as "public enemy number one in the United States." But it was a straw man. John Ehrlichman, counsel and assistant to President Nixon (and a Watergate co-conspirator), later explained what was really going on. "The Nixon campaign in 1968, and the Nixon White House after that, had two enemies: the anti-war left and black people. . . . We knew we couldn't make it illegal to be either against the war or black, but by getting the public to associate the hippies with marijuana and blacks with heroin, and then criminalizing both heavily, we could disrupt those communities. We could arrest their leaders, raid their homes, break up their meetings, and vilify them night after night on the evening news. Did we know we were lying about the drugs? Of course we did."

It was President Bill Clinton who introduced the three-strikes rule and tougher sentencing for drug crimes. He was singlehandedly responsible for introducing the largest crime bill in U.S. history and exploding the size of the prison population, creating the epidemic of mass incarceration. Similarly, in Canada, while the Stephen Harper Conservative government increased the number of offences carrying mandatory minimums with wild abandon, the subsequent Liberal government of Justin Trudeau did nothing to unwind them and even passed all sorts of regressive criminal law legislation under the guise of social sensitivity. It is indeed ironic that one of the few presidents in the United States who has considered any type of prison reform, even though it is a woefully modest one, is none other than Donald Trump.

Politicians are also quick to endorse a tough-on-crime mantra because it is convenient, and also cheap. It costs next to nothing to pass legislation, and by doing so they signal to the electorate that they're serious about protecting us from criminals. This is also a Trojan horse. More criminalization gives the public false comfort that politicians are responding to their concerns without any real sweat equity on the part of those politicians.

This bait-and-switch game that politicians like to play when it comes to justice reform has been made easier for them by the worrying rise of populism. The placement of the judiciary in the democratic hierarchy has always been somewhat fragile. Tensions between elected officials in the executive branch of government and the judicial branch have always existed because the judicial branch can exercise an override on a politician's desire to do whatever they want—or what they refer to as "the will of the people."

This is how it works in its most rudimentary form. Politicians pass laws. Members of the public can challenge those laws as infringing on rights or being beyond the scope of the elected lawmaker. The courts then review the dispute and make a determination. If the lawmaker is unhappy with the result, then they have every right to go back to the drawing board and to draft something that is consistent with the law or the constitution. And if you as a member of the public think that the new legislation still trounces rights, then back to the courts you go.

Our judges are often accused of writing or rewriting our laws. Judges do not do this, although in the scope of determining legal disputes, they routinely do interpret laws and give content and breadth where the words alone do not capture the full scope of the meaning or right at issue. This does not turn judges into de facto legislators. Giving meaning to the legislators' words is a necessary byproduct of legal or constitutional interpretation. Elected officials do not trump judges, and judges do not trump elected officials. Every actor has their own lane, and if they are doing their job properly, they should stay in that lane. Judges attuned to their role generally do not have a great deal of trouble playing by the rules. If they step astray, they are readily corrected by an appellate court. It's the politicians that can't quite figure out the rules of the road.

Governments, while purporting to be representative, do not actually like being held accountable to anyone but those who have elected them, and so they routinely decry "activist" judges. A judge can tell a government what it can and cannot do because it is the job of the courts to interpret the laws that are passed, to ensure constitutional rights are protected, and to ensure that the government (at whatever level) has the legal authority to pass that law.

Nevertheless, there is a range of views about what the proper role of a judge is. Some argue that a judge should not veer from what is on the page in black and white. In its crudest form, the role of judges is to strictly interpret the constitution by divining the original intent of its drafters unconnected to modern-day society. Current context is irrelevant, as are changes in our thinking and society. They ascribe to a view that the law is static, interpretation must be faithful to original intent, and any changes are to come only from elected representatives. Restraint is the mantra. At the other end of the spectrum are those that view law in general, and the constitution in particular, as connected to and responsive to current society. Within this paradigm, the judge, when interpreting laws, must apply this contextual analysis and not be constrained only by the words on the page or the framers' original intent.

That is the spectrum in its rather basic form. Generally, the judgment is driven by the approach the particular judge takes to the fundamental task of constitutional and statutory interpretation, not whether they are "activists" trying to trounce the rules of elected officials.

These sorts of debates are not new, because situating the judiciary—a largely non-democratic institution—as the guardian of democratic values is understandably at times confusing to the public and, it appears, increasingly so to the politicians, whose rising autocratic thinking leads them to conclude that they and only they are the arbiters of the will of the people. Any obstruction of their political fiat, judicial or otherwise, is seen as a challenge to their legitimacy. President Trump is a case in point, but Canadian politicians are hardly innocent in this regard. Ontario premier Doug Ford, after a defeat in the court system, decried the legitimacy of judges because "I was elected. The judge was appointed." This of course fundamentally misconceives the nature of our constitutional democracy. But what was more worrying is that politicians across Canada joined the premier's chorus.

The result is that sometimes there is a strained relationship between those who are elected and seek to impose the will of the majority, and the judiciary, who check the unlawful power of elected officials and must accord protection to the rights of the minority. This natural tension is not unhealthy. It is necessary both to a meaningful democracy and to foster public dialogue. It has the consequence of constantly checking how we have chosen to organize ourselves in a democratic society and, most importantly, requires constant affirmation that we are on the correct path. It is this reaffirmation that is currently waning because it has been replaced by an either/or proposition. You're either with the elected officials or you are with the judges.

Recently, we have witnessed a turn of events. Historically, we have valued the justice system as unassailable and unsullied by the messiness of politics. The shift away from this view in the last four or five years is not about the preservation of democratic institutions. Or meaningful debate. Or indeed accountability, a word that is kicked around with wild abandon without anyone ever asking exactly *who* these institutions are supposed to be accountable to. There is an all-out attack on the justice system, the judiciary and the lawyers who participate in the system. These types of attacks have a long history in virtually every autocratic regime you can think of, from Russia to China to Turkey. Look to any autocracy or sham democratic state and you will see that they have thrived only by suppressing an independent judiciary and bar, sources of legitimate challenge to politicians. The subtle erosion of these legal institutions is a necessary step in the march to consolidate autocratic power.

The result is that the long-running tension between the political arm of government and the judiciary has moved forums. Given the sacrosanct rule that judges cannot generally comment out of court, must speak through their judgments and should never engage in public debate, who do you think is winning in the public eye? The Tweeters in Chief, of course.

On Friday, January 29, 2018, President Trump issued an executive order banning from the U.S. people from seven countries for the purpose of "protecting the nation from foreign terrorists." Let's put aside for a moment the fact that the new vetting measures excluded refugees fleeing war-torn nations, and that the ban also applied to people who had green cards, and that there was no evidence that this ban would make anyone safer given that not one of those seven countries had been responsible for a terrorist act on American soil. And for those who believe in the sovereignty of countries on the list, the right of the executive to make policy choices and the desire for a stricter immigration policy, let's park that view as well. There are legitimate debates on immigration policies and what is and is not effective. The lesson here isn't about the merits of what is a legitimate debate but rather about *how* that debate was carried out.

The ban found its way into a courtroom, where a judge, appointed by a Republican president, imposed an interim suspension of it. This was welcome news to some—but not all. Upon hearing the news, there was one person who went ballistic. And he made his displeasure known publicly. The president of the United States immediately took to Twitter with a litany of attacks on the judge: "The opinion of this so-called judge, which essentially takes law-enforcement away from our country, is ridiculous and will be overturned!" "Because the ban was lifted by a judge, many very bad and dangerous people may be pouring into our country. A terrible decision." "What is our country coming to when a judge can halt a Homeland Security travel ban and anyone, even with bad intentions, can come into U.S.?" "I have instructed Homeland Security to check people coming into our country VERY CAREFULLY. The courts are making the job very difficult!" "Just cannot believe a judge would put our country in such peril. If something happens blame him and court system. People pouring in. Bad!" "The judge opens up our country to potential terrorists and others that do not have our best interests at heart. Bad people are very happy!"

Calling a judge a "so-called judge" is not just an insult; nor is it merely a complaint about a judge Donald Trump disagrees with. It is statement from the president of the United States that a person whose position demands they be judicial and judicious is not. It is an attempt to delegitimize the judicial institution.

When a leader asks in a tweet what our country is coming to when a judge can overrule the government, the leader questions the very constitutional core of a democracy and the inherent and independent checks and balances that are foundational principles. It is the role of courts to ensure that the government always acts consistent with the constitution and the laws of the country. It is at the heart of a democracy that the rights of individuals cannot be taken away, even by majority vote, and that the minority are protected.

The president of the United States said that a judge had put the country in peril, and if something happened (the "something" that he not so subtly alluded to was a terrorist attack), then the judge and the court system were to blame. The accusations here are, first, that the judge and the judiciary do not have the best interests of the citizens at heart, and, second, that they dared to second-guess the executive. Trump's tweets resulted in the judge having to obtain a security detail because of the many threats he began receiving.

The message that Trump was sending to the public was that he, not the judiciary, had the people's best interests at heart. The judiciary, and by extension the justice system, are to be viewed with suspicion, as being unconnected and out of touch with the proverbial common man. Delegitimizing the justice system is a winning strategy for anyone seeking to consolidate power, and it's happening more and more these days in democratic countries around the world.

Judicial rulings are criticized all the time. They always have been, and they should be. But there is a difference between criticizing a ruling and personally attacking a judge. Even more important is who is doing the criticizing. Not all critics are the same. Every political leader has a special platform and authority, and therefore a unique responsibility not to undermine the judicial branch. And yet they continue to do so with alarming frequency these days.

In the United States, where judges are often elected, massive campaigns are run to prevent their re-election. The attacks virtually always turn on the judge's conviction record. The Brennan Center for Justice, in a review of judicial selection in state courts, concluded that millions of dollars are spent on negative ads that characterize candidates as issuing lenient sentences and failing to protect women and children. The fascinating thing is who is running these "soft on crime" ads. They are generally organizations that don't have any skin in the game. For example, one of the nastiest ads in 2014 was seen in North Carolina and characterized a sitting judge as a person who "sides with child predators" because of a decision that monitoring bracelets could not be imposed after a defendant had already been sentenced. The ad was sponsored by two tobacco companies that were frequent litigants in that court and did not want this judge re-elected. It was judge-shopping, not principle, that was the driver. In West Virginia, a mining company ran a "for the sake of the kids" anti-judge ad. In Iowa, ads were directed at liberal judges who had voted in favour of same-sex rights.

What *do* we expect judges to be accountable to? The impartial and objective application and analysis of the law. To quote Aristotle: reason unaffected by desire. Judicial independence is not contrary to judicial accountability. Judicial accountability is found through open courts, the ability of the public and media to criticize decisions, social-context education provided to judges, professional discipline of judges, and, most significantly, the appellate process.

If we want judges to depend upon majority approval, the system will inevitably collapse because courts will simply be unable to perform one of their most important roles: being, in the words of U.S. Supreme Court Justice Hugo Black, "havens of refuge for those who might otherwise suffer because they are helpless, weak, outnumbered, or because they are nonconforming victims of prejudice and public excitement." The English philosopher John Locke said that judicial independence ensures that the law would not "be varied in particular cases but [be the same] for rich and poor, for the favourite at court and the country man at plough." Judges are accountable to all of us and we ensure accountability by protecting their independence from any and all inteference, including that of politicans or the call of the majority.

This brings us back to the beginning. The challenge to or erosion of the presumption of innocence—and our legal system in general—stems from how we are currently discussing these things, which is frequently online, quickly, impatiently, and with not enough facts and analysis at hand.

A meaningful conversation requires context. And context can only come from not only knowing our history but also understanding the present and looking towards the future to inform our expectations of and aspirations for the legal system.

Our rights aren't like a light switch. You can't turn them off when they're inconvenient and back on when they are. If you want to live in the light, it means that as a society we must withstand its uncomfortable glare. It means that the light comes on for everyone, no matter the offence, no matter the offender, and that sometimes is uncomfortable. A principled extension of constitutional protections such as the presumption of innocence and a fair hearing, even when we are shocked by the crime or dislike the offender, is the most challenging part of the justice system. Chipping away at these things threatens the core of the institution.

It should not take wrongful conviction after wrongful conviction to remind us that we are human, that we get it wrong when we let our guard down, when we become complacent or lazy or distracted from the sole function of the justice system. We cannot afford—nor do we have the luxury of—compromise here. The justice system shouldn't be so easily dismantled by popularity contests or political votes or populist sentiment.

It is easy to extend rights to the virtuous, but the challenge of a democracy is to extend those same rights to everyone, whether or not you agree with them or like them. And it should be remembered that the virtuous—Nelson Mandela, for example—was far from being considered virtuous at the time of his prosecution. Ronald Reagan called the African National Congress "terrorists" and called apartheid "a tribal policy more than it is a racial policy."

So what do we do? Extend every right, every protection, to Nelson Mandela but not to a fifteen-year-old boy charged with terrorism offences? Do we extend those rights to pro-choice doctors, knowing that many anti-abortion states in the United States would not? Who decides who is entitled to the protection of the law and when? Only after they have been exonerated or lauded as visionary or regarded as virtuous?

It is astounding to me how we keep forgetting about countries where people are prosecuted because they are poor, marginalized, unpopular, where people are prosecuted for their sexual orientation, where women are charged for making a complaint, where witnesses are believed because of who they are or disbelieved because of who they are. The one single thread that connects these injustices is a system that does not hold the state to account—that is not principled and committed to its principles no matter how inconvenient that may be. A corrupt justice system always turns on the weak, the fragile and the unpopular.

We are exposed when we forget these lessons. When we adjudicate by popular vote, when we allow public assumptions and presumptions and expectations to infect the legal system, we risk undermining the very essence of our justice system. We risk cutting off the Sphinx's nose to spite our face.

AN END,
OF SORTS

12

EXCUSE MY DUST

ON AUGUST 20, in the early-morning hours, I turned fifty.
I had heard of this happening to others but, honestly, I thought
it would never happen to me. It should have been a happy or at
least neutral milestone. It was neither. Fashion victims such as
myself have a tough time aging gracefully. It's not helped by
the fact that a woman's worth has yet to be measured by her
life achievements or her battle scars. I wish it were different, but

it is not. I'd like to give an uplifting, life-affirming message about the whole thing, or claim that it didn't affect me in the least, that we should just "own" it all, but that wouldn't be true. The self-care anti-aging industry aimed at suckers like me doesn't help, and the fact that we are encouraged to lie about our age can only mean that it is a number best kept hidden from public view. Which of course is why I've decided to spend an entire chapter writing about it. That way, there can be no mistake. I'm fifty. Well over, actually.

I wasn't alone in my reaction to hitting fifty. Most of my friends, male and female, were on the precipice of their sixth decade, though it was glaringly obvious that the significance of this birthday differed depending on gender. I couldn't help but notice that my male friends were celebrating with wild abandon, as though they had just reached a moment in their life that, in fact, deserved celebration. Who could blame them? According to various analytics, men hit their prime at fifty. My analytics were far less cheerful.

I did my best to elegantly survive this birthday through collective therapy with my female friends who were quietly, some more stoically than others, suffering along with me. A few naive optimists in our group insisted on trumpeting all the great things that we had accomplished in our lives. I hate those glass-half-full people, although even they were scouring the internet the day after their birthday for the newest wrinkle-eradicating miracle. It is not unusual for me to receive an email from one of these friends with the subject line: URGENT—BUY THIS RIGHT NOW. We've actually done collective online cosmetics shops, where we sit down, call out our latest face-saving discovery and do a cult-like mass online order. I've never walked into a cosmetics department without believing that the product I am about to buy is the magical elixir for everything that is wrong with me. A face cream is made of whale plasma? Sign me up! I will slap it on if it will help.

I know that I really should grin and bear it and not give in to these awful stereotypes that keep knocking at my door, but I just can't. I'm tired of the silly platitudes: *These are your best years. Now you don't have to bother being worried about what you look like. This is the age when you are comfortable in your own skin. Now you can do things on your own terms.* It's all garbage. Why should it take me five decades to get comfortable in my own skin, something the other half of the population gets to do without a second thought? I'm convinced that it's not our fault. Where women properly fit in society at a particular age is a constantly evolving metric. And to be fair, it's hard to figure out where we'd like to be when women are constantly being told where to go.

The one place I unequivocally didn't want to be sent was the faraway neverland of "fifty and over." Not publicly, anyway. I love playing dress-up, and if I could spend my life sitting in a makeup chair, I would. But damn it if everyone wasn't trying to spoil this little bit of fun for me. None of my friends' hopeful platitudes matter a whole lot when I pick up a fashion magazine and see that in the "dressing for your age" section, all women over fifty are lumped into one wholly amorphous, sidelined category. Dressing for your 20s. Dressing for 30s. Dressing for 40s. Dressing for 50s and over. As though once I reached a half-century, all the decades to follow must blend together and my continued existence in them is indistinguishable.

So now, although I did nothing to apply for this particular designation, I'm in the "fifty and over" category in the "dressing for your age" section. I don't even warrant my very own fashion category? Being permanently sidelined to the backwater of these magazines is a hard blow to my ego. It's not as if I've been relegated to a lesser league and can fight my way back—I'm banished there forever. What catastrophe would befall the world, exactly, if a few of us fifty-and-overs forget or, worse still, brazenly choose to dress like the "twenty and over" category? I didn't know and the fashion industry clearly wasn't taking the chance.

Then, just as I was getting ready to attempt to come to terms with aging, I nearly died.

In April of the year of my fifth decade of discontent, my husband and I took a trip to New York City. The day before we went, I had thrown a women-only professional event that invited our colleagues to get manicures and drink booze. Nothing better than alcohol combined with getting your nails done. But I was feeling lousy the entire night, as though I had the flu. When I got home, I went straight to bed, but couldn't lie on my right side without extreme pain. The next morning, I was feeling worse and started coughing up blood. I went to a clinic and they told me that I had likely scratched my throat while coughing and that all I had was a cold. Except I did not have a cold. I don't have a medical degree but I know whether I have a cold or not. It didn't matter, it was a good enough answer for me, so off we went to New York.

I had to drag myself through the first day of the trip, and by that evening, I couldn't even leave the hotel room, which, for me, in New York City, was a sure sign that something was seriously wrong. I was having waves of the most excruciating pain. Think of labour contractions and then magnify by ten. I took Tylenol and some muscle relaxants, but nothing worked, and the waves were coming every ten minutes. Convinced it would pass, I insisted on staying in New York. The next morning, the pain hadn't abated in the slightest, and it was obvious that we needed to get home. I moved our flight up but kept it late enough to allow me to somehow haul myself to Bergdorf Goodman. Bergdorf's is the happiest place on earth for me, and no illness was going to cause me to miss it. I appreciate that this is somewhat pathological and inexplicable, but there are things about all of us that are. For me, shopping is therapeutic *and* I hate admitting that I'm sick. This combination meant that before flying home and checking into a hospital, I *needed* to shop. I pulled myself together long enough to buy a suit, but when I couldn't make it through the shoe department, that's when my husband and I really knew I was in trouble. We raced to the airport with me doubled over in pain.

Twenty-four hours later, diagnosed with a pulmonary embolism, I resisted the morphine that the doctor was trying to force-feed me. I told him that I could handle the pain, but the glaring light in the hospital and the colour of the gown were killing me. I checked myself out early, certain that it would all be a distant memory once I got home. I wound up back in the hospital the next day. Fortunately, they figured out what medication would work, and I was sent home on bedrest for a few weeks. I crawled into the office two days later, convinced that nobody would notice I looked green. My partner Scott did and insisted that if I did not go home immediately, he would officially dissolve our partnership. I went home. But two days later, when I realized that I had begun scheduling my entire day by what time *Ellen* or *Oprah* came on, I went back to work. Being down for the count makes me angry.

All in all, there was no way that turning fifty, post-near-death experience, was going to be elegant.

I couldn't help but wonder, if that clot had completed its little mission, would I have literally dropped dead in Bergdorf's? I mean, if you've got to go, it's as good a place as any. I think this is an entirely sensible final resting place. I'd like my ashes to be dispersed in the shoe department but only during the fall season, because fall palettes work much better for me, even my ashes.

A sensible person, after a brush with death, might re-evaluate their priorities. A wake-up call of sorts. I know other people who have had similar experiences and they tell me that their health crisis caused them to let go of the small stuff and focus on "what's really important." Very few things are more important to me than collagen regeneration and fighting the eternal battle against hyperpigmentation (a late-breaking age-related gift, ladies). The blood coursing through my veins is thinner now courtesy of blood thinners, but I am still clutching my VIB Sephora card as if my life depended on it—and it does. The truth is, I am more concerned about highlighting my cheekbones than I ever was about death.

In the end, I knew I was supposed to grin and bear the whole turning-fifty thing, so I did what I had to do. I put my head down and had a birthday dinner with my loved ones. I had a celebratory drink with my friends to mark the occasion, and my office threw me a lovely surprise party. And there it was. I was fifty. Woohoo!

I know that young women are saying things like fifty is the new forty, but I liked the old thirty—what the hell was wrong with that? And to make matters worse, I couldn't help but notice that for my male friends celebrating their fiftieth, the event was just short of throwing a military parade. Kids, check. Fancy cars, check. Career, check. Good wife, check. An older, age-appropriate wife means that the male gets credit for having tolerated a lengthy and successful marriage. This display of manly marital forbearance is usually accompanied by a joke about always having to say "yes, dear" and agreeing with your nagging wife. If, however, the man has moved on to wife number two, the younger model, that attests to his ongoing virility and attractiveness. Either way, it's a win-win for him. I wasn't exactly feeling the win-win, I've got to be honest.

Even those of us who have spent our lives trying to avoid aging can't catch a break. Entertainment rags frequently proclaim with surprise and astonishment that women fifty and over are still worth something. "Jennifer Lopez at 50" is something you often see splashed on a front cover. She is superhuman, apparently, and like many of her famous type, they just don't seem to age. A good dose of airbrushing and injections don't hurt either, nor do several hours a day with a personal trainer, but it is an awful lot for the rest of us to try to live up to. I'm not immune to the pull of this fantasy and have been known to call up my dermatologist, who happens to be a friend, and demand that she immediately make me look as good as Jennifer Lopez. When she politely declines and explains there is a lot that goes into "Jennifer Lopez at 50," I begrudgingly accept it—only to ask her again the next time we are on our joint dog walks. "Are you *sure* you can't make me look like Jennifer Lopez?" She just ignores me now.

It's not just me. Older women are valued a little differently. Older women in the entertainment industry routinely discuss being sidelined into mom roles, secondary characters or nonspeaking roles as they are aged out of leading roles. There are a few Meryl Streep-like exceptions, the grande dames of the industry, but they are far too rare and usually treated, for good reason, as anomalies. Here are some data points that paint the picture. An analysis of G-rated films between 1990 and 2005 by the Geena Davis Institute on Gender in Media found that in general, regardless of age, only 28 percent of speaking roles went to female characters. In 2015, just 17 percent of top-grossing films had a female lead. In films with a female lead, women spoke 51 percent of the time, but when the lead was male, women's speaking time dropped to 27 percent, and when a man and a woman were co-leads, women's speaking time rose only to 39 percent. In general, male characters spoke twice as often as female characters in top box office movies. The statistics are exacerbated as women get older. In other words, as women get older, they are silenced— *literally*. They are given fewer lines and recede into the background, supporting role. This is the message being conveyed to women by an industry with outsized influence: be quiet, and quieter still as you age when you become virtually invisible but for the sweat stains from the menopausal hot flashes you suffer through.

There is a lot said about women aging "gracefully," but the fact is we are not allowed to do so. We are spontaneously combusting throughout the whole damn process, and while we do, indignity is heaped upon indignity as we are being put out to pasture. It gives a new meaning to being seen and not heard, whatever your age. But this is not unique to the entertainment industry. Even in my profession, which is not based on personal appearance, where we literally speak for a living, we don't do any better. According to the Bizzabo Blog, in law, 76 percent of those who speak publicly—at conferences and various other forums—are male. A 2004 study of Harvard Law School classrooms found that men were 50 percent more likely than women to volunteer at least one comment during class, and 144 percent more likely to speak voluntarily at least three times. Researchers at the Northwestern Pritzker School of Law analyzed speaking patterns at the Supreme Court of the United States in 1990, 2002, and 2015. In 1990, Justice Sandra Day O'Connor was the only woman among the nine justices. Of all interruptions by colleagues on the bench, she was the recipient of 35.7 percent of them. By 2002, Justice Ruth Bader Ginsburg had become the second justice on the court, and together they faced 45.3 percent of all interruptions. By 2015, there were three women justices—Ginsburg, Sonia Sotomayor and Elena Kagan—and together they faced 65.9 percent of all interruptions. I mean, honestly, if you're going to shut down RBG, do the rest of us have a chance?

Not much, it appears. The most public of the Interrupters, Donald Trump, interrupted Hillary Clinton fifty-one times in a ninety-minute presidential debate in 2016, while she interrupted him only seventeen times. I doubt anyone would think Clinton is a shrinking violet, and yes, Trump is, well, Trumpian, but there is something troubling buried deep in that one statistic. And it cannot be divorced from the fact that Clinton is a woman, and an older woman at that, who spent two elections attempting to find her place, to be relatable, to be sufficiently unthreatening while conveying confidence that she could get the job done. And while the media and public agonized over her hair, whether she shed a tear when talking about her daughter, whether she was feminine enough, whether her clothes were just right, the message was loud and clear: there was something not quite right about that woman, so much so that she was beaten by a woefully underqualified, hyperaggressive Oompa Loompa. Too bad she didn't look quite right for her age. Ahh, if only she'd gotten the colour of her pantsuits correct, just think where the world would be now.

Here's the point. When some of the most respected and well-known women in the world, from high-profile actresses to Supreme Court justices to politicians, can be sidelined and silenced in such a public way, what do we expect young women to take away from that?

I survived turning fifty—obviously, because I'm writing this. I admit that I am profoundly fortunate. I have great friends. I have my wonderful family. I have a fulfilling job. I consoled myself by believing that no one outside of those closest to me ever needed to know that I was that awful number. But oh, how wrong I was.

I had no idea of what was coming a few months later, when a trial I was involved in got more than a little media attention—when my name would officially be changed from "Marie Henein" to "Marie Henein for 50." I would have the distinct privilege of having my age mentioned over and over and over again in numerous articles and interviews. As if that wasn't nauseating enough, the Twitterati jumped in with all sorts of commentary on my age as well as my looks. You know when people talk about "they" and you ask who "they" is?

Well, the proverbial "they" has found a comfortable home on Twitter—an anonymous, cacophonous, obnoxious blob of They. Anyway, *they* swung into action. My favourite was the body rub parlour that tweeted "Marie Henein is kinda hot." *Kinda?* That was unnecessarily mean and dismissive I thought—for a body rub parlour. A fifty-year-old clearly wasn't going to make the cut, not even for a body rub parlour. I was doomed.

Nowadays, seeking some kind of external validation, my only fix is being trolled by an elderly male lawyer whom I often see in a particular courthouse. Every time we bump into each other, he corners me, gets awfully close and says the very same thing because he keeps forgetting that we've met before. "Marie Henein," he says, "it is such an honour to meet you. Your brains are exceeded only by your beauty." And I always reply, "Well thank god I have my brains, because the looks are going." He smiles and has no clue what I'm talking about. I think he is trying to be kind. I confess that since I've turned fifty, I actually go looking for him in the courthouse. At least I can count on him to give me a backhanded compliment. Now if only I could convince him that my brains were more important than my looks.

Amazonian efforts are being undertaken to reverse the ageist tide, to encourage women to feel positive about themselves. Bravo to these heroic efforts to convey age-positive imagery and empowerment, to stamp out ageism, to reorient to the real value of half the world's population, to not fall into the sexist ideals, to unchain ourselves from, well, from what exactly? Society, it seems. And that is the real problem. We women still live *here*. *Hot . . . for fifty* is living right here. The misanthrope in me wonders, When exactly did it become *my* problem, *our* problem to fix? We didn't create it, and we sure as hell don't impose it.

We can feel as good as we want about ourselves, but until the valuation metric for females is changed, until Hillary and RBG aren't silenced, until public female figures are judged on their capability rather than whether they are looking fresh that day, until then we will find only modest relief, in the echo chamber while we clap each other on the back. The rest of the world needs to join in on the applause.

So here's the message. Loud and clear. I felt lousy turning fifty. I didn't feel an empowered *carpe diem* moment and I think I, we, should have. The truth is, I'm a pretty tough broad, but the whole thing got to me. It all got to Hillary Clinton, who disappeared into the wilderness for months after her defeat, and even then the commentary was still about how she looked awful because her hair hadn't been done. I'm sure it got to RBG and Margaret Thatcher and my mom and virtually every other woman. I certainly don't have a panacea to solve it. I don't have an uplifting "you will overcome" self-help message, in case you hadn't noticed.

I *do* have a message for the sideliners, though. Perhaps, just maybe, you could kindly keep your opinions to yourself, and I will dress for any age I choose, look whatever way I want, say what I wish, anti-age or age, be a nasty woman or not, without explanation or excuse.

For now, I'm slapping glitter on my fifty-year-old face hoping that it shaves ten years off. I'd snort it if I could, just to have glitter coursing through my veins. And maybe next time, you might want to write, "Marie Henein . . . hot for any age."

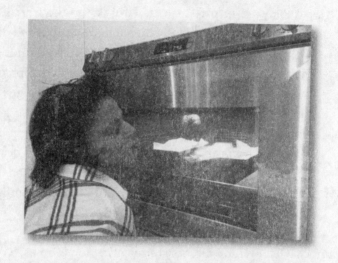

13

SHE MAKES A MEAN BEEF STROGANOFF

WE WOMEN ARE NEVER QUITE RIGHT. A little too much of this, not enough of that. Perpetually in need of tweaking. If we could just tone down, speak up, be more assertive, know our place, be slightly less ambitious or shrill, dress less provocatively, look more feminine, be thinner, heavier—we would be perfect! Of course, none of us can measure up, but damn us all if we don't spend our lives trying.

Society has a pathological compulsion to provide the female sex with endless direction and guidance under the guise of friendly and helpful advice. Why everyone is consumed with making us over, rather than focusing on themselves, defies rational explanation, but this persistent human pathology is in part fuelled, I think, by the fear that if the female sex is not constantly directed, discussed, and dissected, we will go off the rails, maybe even become unhinged and inevitably upend the world order. Religions are preoccupied with keeping us in our place, and political campaigns are won or lost on how to control our bodies. We are up for grabs. We won the vote, but make no mistake, we are still being bartered. Leaders have been made and broken by striking deals about us—to ensure an anti-abortion court, to defund Planned Parenthood, to return to good old traditional family values. "Family" values aren't about families at all. They are about women and where we belong.

And yet, despite this unrelenting focus on us, women are widely under-represented in politics, art, science, law . . . in virtually every facet of professional life. This under-representation is explained away by silly theories about either our inherent limitations or our natural "maternal" dispositions that somehow make us unqualified. Either we are coddled by the sensitive feminist male who, so dazzled by his own new-found sensitivity, feels that women must be infantilized, lest we have a sudden onset of the vapours and faint, or we are subjected to the howls of the blatant misogynist who feels his masculinity is under siege by our every move. Neither group is doing us any good.

What I do know is that most women I have met are tough. And not one of them is plotting the takedown or, for that matter, seeking the protection of the opposite sex. We must start here: we are not in need of fixing. We are in need of a runway, some good old-fashioned space to do our thing.

From popular movies to books, from politics to religion, and in the media, the through-line is correction and adjustment. So who can blame young women for being obsessed with their own inadequacies when everyone else is? The message is clear—any right-thinking woman should understand her inherent, natural deficiencies and immediately set off on a lifelong journey of self-discovery and inevitable self-improvement, and probably forgo external things such as the world, life, and work. A trip to the women's self-help section of your local bookstore tells you all you need to know: *Women Who Think Too Much: How to Break Free of Overthinking and Reclaim Your Life*; *Choosing ME before WE: Every Woman's Guide to Life and Love*; *The Gifts of Imperfection: Let Go of Who You Think You're Supposed to Be and Embrace Who You Are*; *Nice Girls Don't Get the Corner Office: 101 Unconscious Mistakes That Women Make That Sabotage Their Careers*; *The Universe Has Your Back: Transform Fear to Faith*; *I Shouldn't Be Telling You This: How to Ask for the Money, Snag the Promotion, and Create the Career You Deserve*; *How to Be a Person in the World: Ask Polly's Guide through the Paradoxes of Modern Life* and of course the mega-bestseller *Lean In: Women, Work and the Will to Lead*. Compare that with the men's self-help section: *Fire in the Belly: On Being a Man*; *The 48 Laws of Power*; *Think and Grow Rich*. Men are to be reminded of their inner strength and superiority, while women need to be taught how to overcome their inherent, life-stunting limitations.

This phenomenon has managed to cripple half the world's population, to preclude large numbers of women around the world from getting a proper education or being able to live life with any independence. Think of this fact alone: approximately 14 million women in Saudi Arabia cannot leave their houses without the permission of their husbands. Women are enslaved in that country, and yet world leaders do billions of dollars of business with it every year. Closer to home, in the United States, a mere 1.7 percent of women in the workforce earn the same as or more than their male counterparts. Women of colour make up only 5 percent of senior executive positions, and only about 12 percent earn college degrees. I can fill pages with these kinds of statistics from anywhere in the world. We are all losers because we have done our level best to constrain, silence and stifle half of the world's talent. The sheer basic economics of this persistent inequality make it incomprehensible.

External success, at least the male kind, is available for women only if it is served up with a good dose of mush or maternal instinct to soften the blow and explain the anomaly. Why else, when I'm interviewed, am I asked to confirm that I have children, whether I am a good mother, whether I am married and how I "balance" it all? As though being a lawyer and a mother are mutually exclusive or interrelated. That question ignores the obvious fact that women all over the world work to support themselves and their families in far tougher jobs than mine. These questions do not get asked when my male colleagues are interviewed because, I am sure, no one has ever wondered how it was possible for them to be professionals and fathers as well. The two concepts—a work life and a personal life—are not presumptively on a collision course for the male sex. The not-so-subtle implication for women is obvious. When I am asked "How can you do it all?" or "Are you a mother?" what I am really being asked is, "Are you any good at either? Which is suffering? Where have you fallen short? What have you chosen? Work? Then you are a bad mother. Family? Then you must be uncommitted to your profession."

I recall attending an induction ceremony into the American College of Trial Lawyers, a prestigious North American organization that requires a vetting process and then an invitation to join. The membership was an impressive array of talented litigators, but largely white and male in constitution and hence leadership. Since being founded in 1950, and approximately sixty-eight presidents later, this was the first president to be female. I recall this appointment because it was historic—a moment demonstrating that this old institution of male lawyers was perhaps becoming more gender-inclusive. Unfortunately, much of the new president's acceptance speech was about how humble and grateful she was to be bestowed this honour. This is a common occurrence for women who achieve a semblance of success, particularly if that involves assuming a position usually reserved for the male sex. Rather than beating her chest and reminding everyone how historic the moment was, and how shameful it was that it took more than half a century to find one female lawyer worthy to lead, she was elegantly demure, grateful, and sufficiently deferential so as not to offend. It is the Hillary Clinton predicament, and I can't say I blame her. Female pioneers have always had to tread lightly in new territory so as not to ruffle too many feathers, to ensure our interloping is tolerable.

At the black-tie ceremony where I was inducted as a member, I was with my husband, sitting beside another inductee and his wife. After regaling us with stories of her husband's professional success, the wife turned to me and said that I too must be brimming with pride at my husband's accomplishments. I responded that I was extremely proud of him, almost, in fact, as much as he was of me since I was the one being inducted into the college. Her face dropped, but without missing a beat she asked *how* I could be a lawyer *and* a mother. I responded that I hadn't thought about it, but perhaps she might ask her husband, who, apparently, had managed to miraculously be both a lawyer *and* a father. The rest of our dinner was awfully silent.

When women are asked "How can you have it all?," let's be very clear: nobody cares a whit if you have it all. That question isn't designed to assess your competence or measure your fulfillment. The real entreaty is "How can you *do* it all?" And underneath that is the not so obvious judgment: How can you be an amazing mother *and* superstar professional? How can you heal yourself? Heal the men in your world? Lean in. Lean out. Stand up. Sit down. Tell us where you have failed because we know, as a matter of logic, that it is impossible to "do it all."

So when you're asked "How can you do it all?" the real question is "What have you *not* done?" Asking the question is designed to point out the failure. We have failed in our blind embrace of the poisonous balancing myth. In part, I blame Martha Stewart.

Sometime around the late 1990s, I bought my first issue of *Martha Stewart Living*. I would come home exhausted after a stressful day of work and there she was waiting for me. She and I would snuggle together in bed. Martha was always there for me, showing me all the useful things I could be doing if only I wasn't wasting my time on work. Deep down, maybe I wanted to be her, the flawless, unflappable hostess, but that was before I decided it would have been better to actually be Martha Stewart the powerful CEO, or at least represent her when she was criminally charged. These were the early, halcyon days, though. She and I were still in the honeymoon phase of our relationship. I loved her back then, but I should've known, the relationship was doomed from the start.

The magazine promised a new world of personal fulfillment that I hadn't even thought of. I could dazzle family and friends with everything homemade—from labels to cookies, from place settings to hostess gifts; you name it, I could do it. A perfect house, garden, kitchen, and table—and go to court too! While I flipped through *Living*, my deeply ingrained values were being stripped away like the layers of a perfectly refinished Martha Stewart table. I was not the only sucker to buy into this dream that I didn't know I had. The nineties was the decade this uber-domesticity took hold. Women could— *should*—make everything perfect and be house-proud. In my group, dinner parties were a blood sport thrown with wild abandon, often by female professionals, many of whom had decided that their real calling was to give up work and return to home and kitchen and create the newest, fanciest, most impressive dinner table ever.

Selling domesticity is Martha Stewart's *business*. She is the ultimate professional, businesswoman, and feminist. She *employs* the opposite sex—she does not work for them. If you took a peek behind her stiffly ironed apron, you'd see a staff of hundreds making everything look absolutely perfect. She turned unpaid female labour into a *business*. But most of us

didn't look at what she really was and what she truly repre-
sented. We mortal women bought the fantasy hook, line, and
sinker. We didn't know what was really going on behind that
perfectly set table was a billion-dollar-industry selling the
idea of domesticity to us. And so the myth that we women
need to do it all, *can* do it all, took root. It was no different
than the obnoxious Cinderella story we sell to young girls,
except this fable was being marketed to adult women. We
should've known better. Dangerous domesticity, a rewind to
the 1950s—ladies fussing over table settings, gents in the
living room regaling each other with tales from the office. I
confess I was profoundly confused. I kept wandering between
kitchen and living room and finally concluded that I clearly
did not belong in either. Why didn't Martha tell me that? I
started not to trust her.

In the legal profession, as in many others, there is a startling attrition rate among women. It is well known that,
notwithstanding that women account for at least half of
the law school graduates these days, by the first half-decade
they leave private practice to work in institutional settings,
taking positions as in-house counsel with corporations in
droves, and many leave the practice of law altogether. This
drain of legal talent has been an issue for some time,
prompting law firms and advocacy organizations to create
working groups across the country in an attempt to understand and hopefully stem the female exodus. The most
commonly identified reason for women leaving the field is
that they cannot handle the stress of both work and family.

Implicit in this, at least for women, is that they should be handling both *alone*, or at least with very little help. Did anyone stop to ask themselves how it was that our male colleagues were able for years to manage the startling feat of having a career and a family without being driven from their chosen profession? The answer was obvious: They had help. Enormous help that allowed them the freedom to focus on themselves and their careers.

The various law societies across this country must have been avid fans of Martha Stewart as well. They bought into the myth that women lawyers can—and should—do it all. They just needed to figure out how law firms could assist women in achieving this ultimate goal. The reason that women are leaving the profession in droves, they reasoned, is that we as a legal profession have failed to accommodate them with the right tools to continue to shoulder the majority of all household and family burdens *and* have a career.

With this realization, the conferences and handwringing began. Work–life balance was the new rallying cry. The core of the problem for women in a profession like law is the very word *balance*. There is none. Any attempt to convince women that they can and should meet all obligations on all conceivable fronts is misguided. Of course, there were no comparable male conferences. I refuse on principle to attend or even participate in the myriad work–life balance conferences. I will, however, gladly speak to a roomful of men on how they can adjust *their* work–life balance to accommodate female workloads and success. I haven't been invited to one yet.

Any way you put it, a true balance is impossible. What exactly were the law societies trying to accommodate? They were asking firms to make sure we got home in good time . . .

to cook dinner, have quality time with the family. And the firms continue to think they are giving us a great *accommodation*. What an awful word. Accommodation—as though you are going out of your way, doing someone a favour. Here is a secret: for women, having babies is often a biological function, the same as eating. Yet we do not talk of law firms *accommodating* men's choice to eat by giving them a lunch break. Because we have accepted that people need to eat, it is not mischaracterized as an accommodation. It is a reality. You are not "accommodating" women by giving them the necessary time to have children. You are accepting a biological reality.

The balance myth has not only preoccupied employers; it has most unfortunately added a serious level of stress for women entering the workforce. It is the question I get asked most often by young female lawyers. Not "How do you succeed in this business?" but "How do you balance work and family?" My answer is always the same: You do not. Because there is only one of you and you can only be in one place at one time. When you are at work, that is where your attention is, and sometimes your family suffers as a result. At times, it is your family that requires all of you, and your work must take a back seat. Maybe your partner or someone else has to lend a helping hand so you can have the freedom—so you can be liberated from the delusion that it is possible to create and sustain this balance, and be allowed to focus on what you choose to focus on at that moment. Is it any wonder that over the past few decades stress levels among female professionals continue to soar? Anxieties increase and feelings of insecurity grow as we pave a compassionate yellow brick road for young females right out of the profession and back into the home.

The calculus assessing the worth of professional women is different. I once read a *New York Times* obituary that began this way: "She made a mean beef stroganoff, followed her husband from job to job, and took eight years off from work to raise three children." The "she" they were talking about was a rocket scientist; not some run-of-the-mill rocket scientist but a world-famous pioneer of rocket propulsion. The woman was literally a *rocket scientist*, a fact that didn't get mentioned until late in the piece. The *Times* would later apologize, but only after a bit of a furor had erupted.

The living have not fared much better. I was at a conference where two former Supreme Court of Canada justices were introduced. Their domestic skills, from the maternal to culinary, figured prominently in both introductions, as if to say to the audience, *It is okay—they've made a mean beef stroganoff and, oh yes, done some lawyering along the way.* Men, on the other hand, are routinely introduced by noting their myriad professional accomplishments, with the standard mention of the accommodating partner who "made it all possible." Behind every man . . .

Male success is different. Unburdened by the need to do it all or manage fatherhood and a professional life, men are free to know that a career and a family are not mutually exclusive. We might want to let our daughters in on this well-guarded little secret.

I recall having a conversation with a male colleague who proudly told me that both his son and daughter were lawyers. He reported that his daughter, having just graduated from law school, had attended an "alternative career day" put on by the law society.

"Why is she already thinking of alternative careers?" I asked him. "She just got here. Shouldn't we give her a chance before telling her she should think of career alternatives?"

"Well," he responded, "so that she could be a mother."

I asked him whether he was concerned about his son being a father and a lawyer without an alternative career. It hadn't occurred to him and, to be fair, it hadn't occurred to the law society either. You can bet that these alternative career days were not being pitched to young male lawyers, counselling them to get out of the profession.

In a prime example of the complete disconnect between what is required and what is given, a number of the Canadian law societies that regulate lawyers decided to offer a "parenting toolkit" to help firms manage the new-found crisis that women sometimes have babies. Here's a letter they suggested managing partners send to pregnant lawyers:

Dear [Name of lawyer]:

On behalf of the partnership of the firm, I would like to congratulate you on the announcement of your new child. This is an important and joyful event.

The firm is committed to assisting parents to get ready for the arrival of their new child, while ensuring that they are not overwhelmed by the challenges of managing their practice. We also want to provide assistance to you while you are on leave and to help you when you return to your practice. We hope to assist you in establishing a good balance between your practice and your family responsibilities.

This New Parent Tool Kit provides you with some of the resources that you will need to get ready for your leave, to enjoy your leave, and to ease back into practice.

Every lawyer who is giving birth will be offered a "Maternity Leave Buddy" to assist her in preparing for her leave, to provide a contact person while she is on leave and to help her return to practice. [Name of lawyer] has been assigned to be your Maternity Leave Buddy. They will be in touch with you in the near future.

If you are not taking a maternity leave but are taking a parental leave and you wish to have a Parental Leave Buddy to assist you to prepare for your leave, stay in contact while on leave, and help with your return to practice, please contact me and we will make the appropriate arrangements.

We look forward to meeting your new arrival and to assisting you with this important event. Again, congratulations.

Yours very truly,
Managing Partner

Throughout the parenting tool kit, the firm is instructed to remind the woman in question that she has an obligation to provide professional services to clients at all times. Thank God. We women lawyers who have had a child tend to forget these things. The kit also offers such helpful advice as telling mothers to keep photos of their child in their office "for personal pleasure and to share"—just in case we weren't sure what baby photographs were for. It goes on to state that the firm will organize "mom luncheons" so that new mothers can discuss their experiences and the stresses they feel. No doubt "dad luncheons," which the law societies seem to have forgotten about, would take on a different tone and purpose.

Reading this tool kit is a better prophylactic than any pill. I cannot describe the many ways that I find this incursion into one's personal life profoundly offensive. The decision to have a child is not a firm-wide catastrophic event. I'm not sure whether the law societies think women are idiots, but if they're looking for a way to further stress them out in a profession that is already loaded with stress, they've found it. The bottom line is that the parent tool kit isn't about parents at all; it is about helping law firms manage an unthinkable crisis—a pregnant lawyer.

Here's the letter I'd like to send:

Dear [Name of lawyer]:

You are having a baby. We are writing to tell you we do not care one way or the other. In our view this is normal, not a catastrophic event that the entire firm has to brace itself for. In fact, it is none of our business what you choose to do in your personal life. We understand that you are probably going to be exhausted for the first trimester and want to kill someone for the rest. We will leave you alone (especially in the last three months) and let you do what you need to do. We've got your back. You are great at what you do. That's why we hired you in the first place. We can hardly wait to see you return. Your baby is awfully lucky to have such a competent mom. And we are awfully lucky to have such a talented lawyer.

Yours very truly,

Managing Partner

PS: We have spoken to your significant other and they understand they have to step up.

The legal community keeps sending the same message to women: professional life is no place for you. And the statistics back that up: while women now make up at least half of law school graduating classes, they account only for approximately 20 percent of law firm partners. The Law Society of Ontario's Justicia Project concluded that many more women than men leave the profession and that work–life balance is the third most oft-identified factor. But it is not the only factor. The greatest male–female gap is found in the upper partner ranges, and it's not hard to figure out why: few women stay around long enough to get there.

As a lawyer, I've decided to keep my focus here on that community—it's what I know and what I experience on a day-to-day basis. But these statistics are mirrored or worse in virtually every other profession: medicine, technology, the entertainment industry, politics. Women are absent in meaningful numbers from positions of power and decision-making. And their attrition rate is almost always significantly higher than that of their male counterparts.

Internal change is the key, though I expect that the catalyst for improvement in the legal profession (or any profession) will be financially driven. Increasingly, corporate clients, when doling out work, look to ensure that there is diversity in the composition of their legal teams. It is insufficient to merely have a few women on the team; the clients paying the bills are demanding women be in the lead partner role—a requirement that many firms will not be able to meet if they continue to fail to actively promote women through the ranks. I recall a friend of mine, a Washington lawyer, telling me how she was recruited from the bench back into private practice when major corporate clients announced that they would no longer deal with law firms that did not reflect diversity in the lead partner managing the file. As a racialized female, the offers to make her partner came fast and furious. As "diversity committees" pop up in firms attempting to fill this gap, the failure to actively promote women and racialized lawyers is the obvious problem—if for nothing more than protecting the bottom line.

We women have an equal obligation not to cede the floor. Education should not be viewed as a luxury, not when young girls around the world are risking their well-being for the mere privilege of going to school or reading a book. We should stop sidelining ourselves.

The notorious silencing of young women in education continues when they move up through our profession—when they sit in boardrooms or in client meetings. A silence driven by the fear of being too loud, too brash, too opinionated, or insufficiently female.

And why is that?

If I hear one more woman talk about "imposter" syndrome—in other words, how it took a long time to recognize their value and worth in the profession—I'm going to scream. I promise you that throughout the history of my profession, and I'm sure most others, not a single acceptance speech ever delivered by our male colleagues ever mentioned imposter syndrome. Not one of those men had a shadow of a doubt that they deserved to be right where they were. No one discussed their beef stroganoff skills. Or their paternal aptitude. Oh, they might thank their mentors along the way, or the people who made it all possible, but none of them, not for a moment, thought they weren't good enough. And yet this is a theme of senior women in any profession. Is it any wonder that young women think it too?

So how *do* you do it all? You don't. You don't have to. Nor should you be expected to. It is easy to "lean in" if you have five nannies helping you out. Most of us don't. So you strike the balance that is comfortable for you. And in all of this, that is for you to decide. Women do not need to be changed, adjusted, domesticated, moulded, formed, or coddled. We need space and a runway. We need others to get out of our way. You know what is better than a feminist leader? A female leader. And if you are in the mood to make a mean beef stroganoff along the way, well that's your call entirely.

14

HOME

MY FATHER CANNOT FATHOM my love of New York City. He has taken to calling me "the New Yorker" (when he isn't calling me "the Downtowner"). "The New Yorker is back in town," he says when I've returned after a trip. Then he follows up with the same question: "Why do you love New York so much?," hoping that maybe one day I will change my answer. But for forty years I've been giving him the same answer. It's a game we play. Maybe if he keeps asking, one day I will surprise him and say something different, like, *I am so happy right here, right where I am.* But I will never say that. Why would I when I know there is always somewhere else to be?

My mom understands the draw of New York, why the din of that bustling city, more than any other, can be soothing to me. She grew up in downtown Cairo and has missed the feeling of it ever since she left. Every few months, I kidnap her so that we can steal away to New York and overdose on fluffy Broadway musicals. I've lost count of how many times we've seen *Fiddler on the Roof.* It doesn't matter, "Sunrise, Sunset" always gets us crying. There is something perversely cathartic about bawling on Broadway right beside people you don't know but who, in that moment, feel the very same emotion as you do. It's a shared experience for a few hours that breeds an odd sense of familiarity and even community, but then just as quickly, the lights come up, the anonymity returns and everybody pours out into the streets. That should be the title of my life in New York: *Bawling on Broadway.*

Even my friends say that the minute I am in the cab crossing the bridge into the city, my whole body relaxes. Where others see mayhem, dirt, confusion, I see beauty and energy, as if my lungs were filling up with the freshest, cleanest air. The grime of New York City is cleansing for me, a mud bath of sorts.

I've tried for a long time to find the place that I am most at home. The courtroom is one, for sure, but I can't say that many other places quite fit the bill. I know that I am probably the happiest in a semi-nomadic state, travelling somewhere new with my family in tow. But I still keep searching, that is the truth. One weekend, for example, convinced that I had failed my children by depriving them of the quintessential northern experience, my husband and I went cottage hunting. And as I stood on a dock, looked around and took in the melodious trill of the loons, I could think only one thing . . . *This. Is. Punitive.* Friends have invited me up to visit them at their beautiful cottages and they know by now that I cannot make it through an entire weekend without escaping back to the city earlier than planned. They have stopped inviting me.

Eventually, I had to concede that if anywhere was going to work, New York was the place. Standing on the corner of Broadway and Forty-Second Street, I am drenched in the lights and breathe in the thick dense air. At night, the low hum of the cars in the streets soothes me to sleep, and in the morning, the beeping and honking tells me when the city is coming to life again, that there are people doing things and that there are things to be done. And maybe it's because I feel a little closer to Sami here, passing by the stores we would go to in the East Village, Trash and Vaudeville, or Maud Frizon on Fifty-Seventh, or walking along Central Park imagining we could afford an apartment there. Can I tell you something? I think sometimes that he must be here in the city, that he's been lying all these years and escaped back to New York and just decided it was best not to tell anyone, even me. I recently stumbled upon the Pyramid Club while I was wandering the streets with my friend Laura. I could not just walk by. We went in, and as soon as we did, I remembered the bar that the drag queens used to get up and dance on, but nothing else felt familiar. "Is this what it was like?" I asked Laura. "It feels smaller." Did I not belong here anymore?

In a city like New York, you can be from anywhere. Everyone is. And no one is ever really *from* New York; we are all foreigners and there is some comfort in that, knowing you are no different from anyone else because everyone is different here. But just as I'm settling in, I inevitably begin to feel restless and need to go back to Toronto. When I return, I am in lower gear. Torontonians are kind and polite. There is an innate decency here that cannot be replicated, but it comes at the cost of losing some edge. In New York, everyone stops and talks to you, but if you are in trouble, they will step right over you. In Toronto, no one will stop and talk to you because that would just be rude, but if you are in trouble, everyone will rush to help you. No place feels just right.

Where are you *really* from?

A few years ago, I was involved in a case that caused all sorts of pundits in the media and on social media to opine on and largely denigrate the justice system. I was relieved and exhausted when it was over. Throughout the trial, as usual, I had refrained from doing any press interviews. My media blackout rule when I am in trial is necessary because the external noise distracts me. My focus has to be on what is happening in the courtroom, because I know what is there. Those parameters are clear. It is only afterwards that I can look around and see what was happening while I was immersed in the trial.

Now, with the trial completed, I watched. There were marches across the country, people actually taking to the streets in opposition to the verdict. Initially, I thought the feverish pitch was bound to die down, but it did not seem to be dying down at all. I kept waiting for people to speak up, to change the dialogue or at least bring some other perspectives, but that wasn't happening much either; social media doesn't afford a lot of breathing room for conversation. Everyone was being excoriated. Taking your fair share of shots comes with the territory when you are a defence lawyer—I've gotten used to that—but what I could not understand was the complete lack of reasoned and calm engagement about the merits and failures of our justice system. And I will tell you this: I was extremely troubled by the conversation, and not because I am opposed to people expressing their opinions or thinking that the justice system needs to be fixed; it was the tone of it all. I felt as though the sky was falling, and so I spent much of the week after the verdict feeling extremely distressed.

Both my law partner Danielle and my husband thought that it was time to do the interview that I had dodged. I tried to convince them that I was not the best person to speak on the matter, that I would be seen as partisan and could not engender the rational discussion about the justice system that I felt was desperately needed. I tried to convince them that perhaps a panel of experts would be more likely to be heard. But both were adamant that it had to be me. I had been asked to do an interview with Peter Mansbridge on his newscast, *The National*. He was prepared to give me the time I thought was necessary to engage in proper conversation about the legal system and to say some things that perhaps the public might want to consider before making up their minds. Mansbridge was a calm, profoundly seasoned interviewer, and most important, he was not sensationalistic. So I reluctantly agreed. I was so reluctant, in fact, that the interview was conducted in my office rather than in a television studio and the network did no advertising until the interview was in the can because of the fear that I would still pull out at the very last minute.

The interview was not done, as I've heard said, "to present my side of the story." There was no "story" to present, and I did not ever view it as me being pitched against the rest of the world. What I wanted to do was provide people with another—informed—perspective about how the justice system works. This does not mean I was unaware of the vitriol directed at me. I tried very hard not to take it personally, although there were times when I unquestionably failed in this regard, but it took discipline and perspective of the external environment. I did this not for self-preservation but because my commitment to all clients required that I navigate through this. While as a lawyer you are front and centre, it is, in the end, in fact not about you. This is why telling "my side of the story" was meaningless. I was not the story. I was the lawyer doing my job. I didn't feel the need to defend myself.

I showed up and did the interview. Danielle stood at the door and watched, and when I walked out, she said it was good, I had said what needed to be said. "I don't think anyone is going to watch this," I responded. After the interview, I didn't feel relief. I was not at all happy to have to say what I was able to say. In fact I was frustrated that any of it needed saying at all. I did not need to get anything off my chest. I did not care that it was a large national audience and, to be honest, I didn't know exactly who would bother to watch. I thought something had to be said and I said it because the institutions that govern our profession, numerous legal organizations, and my colleagues were eerily silent. I felt that the national dialogue was off track and needed perhaps an inside perspective to weigh in. I didn't know if anyone would hear it or take it in, but I hoped some would.

People did. I did not listen when it first aired, and I

learned only through friends that the interview was going to be split over two weekends. When I heard this, I emailed Peter and told him that while I was glad the interview had worked out, I knew that there was definitely one person in Canada who would be extremely grateful if it did not air over two weekends. He elegantly declined my request.

I thought nothing of it until letters started coming in from across the country, from Canadians in the United States, from Canadians stationed in Afghanistan, thanking me for talking about our justice system and for making Canadians feel proud of it.

I'm often asked what the most meaningful moment of my career has been to date. This was it. Not the interview. Not any single case. It was what was *in* those letters that was completely unexpected. One night, I gathered up a few of them and I went to my parents' house. I said that there was something I wanted to show them, something that had happened. We sat around the kitchen table and I pulled the letters out and read aloud: *You are a good Canadian. You represent Canada well. You make me proud of our country.* We didn't say anything for a long time, and then my dad looked at me and said, "This is why we came."

These letters from people I do not know, who only saw me talking about the justice system that I am so proud of, who know me only as a lawyer—they had claimed me for their own, *as* one of their own. People from across this country had said to me that I belong. To them. Here.

Where are you *really* from?

Not from Cairo or Toronto or, as I had long imagined, New York. I know exactly where I am from, where I have always been from.

I am from my Palestinian Teta, my urban Egyptian mother, and my blue-eyed Lebanese father. I am from my beautiful uncle Sami, my funny brother, and my empathetic cousin. I am from my Canadian children and my kind husband and my warrior women friends. I am from my people, from across this country, who claimed me as their own in those letters.

I am still her, that five-year-old girl in that photograph. Did you think I would do it for you now? Stretch out my arms, like my father, cross my legs, let my hips sway to the rhythmic banging of the tablah, sucking the smell of the sweet licorice arak into my lungs with the voices of Fairouz and Oum Kalsoum pounding in my head? Is it time to end the story, my story, this way? No, I will not. Because there are things I still have to say.

Where are you *really* from? I am from the same place as you. I am from them all. I am from wherever I want to be.

15

QUESTIONS MATTER

MINE IS A PROFESSION that studies the art of the question. To lawyers, questions matter. We are aficionados of the well-worded question, spending literally years reading books and attending courses on questioning witnesses. Ask a question one way and you get a certain answer. Change the words up and you can elicit a completely different answer. Even the order in which questions are asked can influence the answers. Every trial lawyer knows the sinking feeling of having asked the wrong question, or one question too many, or the question that invites the devastating answer from the witness, an answer that feels like a body blow and which you spend years replaying. *If only I'd used different words.*

In a courtroom, the power of a question is self-evident. So much so that judges are obliged to remind the jury that a lawyer's questions are not evidence. But they are not inconsequential either. That is precisely why the warning is necessary. It is easy for a layperson to believe a question and an answer have the same evidentiary value. They do not, but a skilful advocate can use a question to convey a theory, a narrative or a point of view. Good lawyers know the importance of a well-phrased question.

Judges, too, determine and define the scope of their judgments by framing the question they are answering in a case. A judgment will often begin with the judge stating the specific question that the judgment is meant to address, signalling the questions the judge has chosen to leave unanswered for another day. We have a legal term for this: *obiter dicta*. Translated, it means "other things said." When a lawyer references *obiter dicta* in a judgment, it means that these judicial statements were made in passing by the judge and not related to the question before the court. They are, therefore, accorded less precedential value.

Questions matter. So it was no surprise that I was transfixed by the Senate questioning of United States Supreme Court nominee Ketanji Brown Jackson. I was admittedly curious as to how the senators would deal with the first Black woman ever nominated to this position in the United States. What were they going to convey to the public watching this moment so intently? The happy ending to this story is that Judge Jackson was confirmed and will be elevated to the Supreme Court. The not-so-happy part of the story is what happened on the road to her confirmation. Voltaire cautioned, "Judge a man by his questions rather than his answers." Indeed, the Senate hearings revealed a great deal about the men and women asking questions. Watching, I could not shake the feeling that something more than Judge Jackson's nomination was at stake.

As is the practice in the United States, a Supreme Court nominee must be subjected to hearings in which senators are given the opportunity to ask questions, ostensibly to assess the nominee's fitness to hold the highest judicial office in the country. I say "subjected" because if you watched even a few moments of the hearings, there is no other word to describe what was on display. The hearings are public, presumably because they are designed to educate and inform citizens about the process. I say "presumably" because you could not discern any attempt to educate or inform the public in any of the questions asked. You surely could not miss one fact: the senators certainly knew the power of their questions—they had clearly spent time crafting them. This was not happenstance. It was deliberate and methodical. There was a purpose in mind.

Judge Jackson was asked myriad questions that appeared to ask one thing but clearly meant another. For example, would she accept that a fetus feels pain at twenty weeks? In other words, was she prepared to overturn *Roe v. Wade*? Did she subscribe to critical race theory? In other words, Was she still going to be Black when she was on the Supreme Court? And could she define the word *woman*? She is one, of course, and so she might know a thing or two about it. But that wasn't really the question. The real question was, How did she define gender and where did she stand exactly when it came to transgender rights? That Judge Jackson did not lose her composure and storm out of the hearings is reason enough to elevate her to the highest court in the land—hell, in the galaxy, for that matter. In the days of haranguing, save for the odd perplexed look, she sat stone-faced and showed restraint, a necessary qualification for any judge.

All these questions were designed to expose which way a judge would rule on the very issues that are likely to soon come before the U.S. Supreme Court. The thing is, though, that judges aren't supposed to rule in the abstract. They are required to set aside their own personal views and apply the law. In a democracy, judicial prejudgment is the very antithesis of what we strive for. As a society, we want in the courts objectivity and open-mindedness and a judge who, notwithstanding their personal views and experience, will determine a case based solely on the evidence and judicial precedent. Most people would want that type of person in their justice system. Not the senators, apparently.

Although Judge Jackson repeatedly attempted to remind the senators of the role of a judge in a democratic system and the importance of deciding cases on the evidence and not prejudging, these basic principles—principles that are foundational to democracy—were lost on the senators. I guess what they really wanted to know was if they could have a Supreme Court judge's vote in the bag. If they could count on her to vote the *right* way, that is, *their* way. There are of course legal systems like that, where a judge is in the pocket of politicians, where you can count on a judge to vote the way a leader wants them to vote. They are found in China and Russia and numerous other autocratic countries.

The methodical dismantling of an independent judiciary is a tried-and-true, indeed necessary, step to consolidating political power. Hungary's Prime Minister Viktor Orbán is a case in point. Orbán has waged a decade-long war to erode the independence of the judiciary as he moves Hungary further and further away from democracy. Most recently, he appointed a stalwart supporter, Zsolt András Varga, as president of the

Supreme Court for a nine-year term. Notwithstanding the National Judicial Council's objection that Varga was unqualified and had no courtroom experience, the appointment proceeded. (It is interesting to note that former president Donald Trump similarly appointed a number of judges who various bar associations had concluded were unqualified.)

This was only the most recent move in Orbán's march towards dismantling an independent judiciary. In fact, it began more than a decade earlier, with terminating the mandate of the chief justice of the Supreme Court in 2011, changing the appointment process so that politically appointed Constitutional Court judges could be appointed to the regular courts, and lowering the retirement age of judges, which allowed Orbán to get rid of at least a third of the judiciary. The European Commission's 2020 Rule of Law Report found that judicial independence in Hungary was a "source of concern." In addition, the report found that "judges and lawyers are subject to negative narratives in the media." In several press statements since 2020, the Hungarian government and pro-government media outlets criticized judicial decisions, particularly those releasing convicts on parole or ruling in favour of inmates who complained about their detention conditions. If there is a way to attempt to show that a judge is unfit, then demonstrating that they are "soft on crime" is a surefire hit. Clearly, the U.S. senators were watching.

A judge's vote that you can count on is *not* something any reasonable person who truly values democracy would want in their judicial system. So why were the senators' questions so intent on conveying to their constituents that knowing if they could count on this judge's vote *was* what the public in a democratic country should want? Or that Judge Jackson's refusal to acquiesce and disclose how she would vote on any particular case was obfuscation?

What they asked about is as telling as how they asked it.

The senators' most sustained attacks on Judge Jackson related to her occupation. Ketanji Brown Jackson, you see, had made a fatal mistake: for some time she had been a defence lawyer—a public defender and appellate counsel. This was where the senatorial attack was most sustained.

Republican Senator Ted Cruz started by bringing up Judge Jackson's law school papers.

As a young law student, Ketanji Brown Jackson had penned a constitutional paper in the *Harvard Law Review* about Megan's Law. We have a similar law in Canada: Christopher's Law. These laws outline what governmental constraints can be imposed on sex offenders after their release from jail for the purpose of public protection. The laws are designed to help track sex offenders after their release. In 1996, when Jackson was writing her law school paper, these laws were new and their constitutionality was very much a subject of academic debate—how far could the state go after an offender has served their time and paid their debt to society in controlling or imposing ongoing or indeterminate constraints? These are complex questions and require a balancing of public protection and individual rights.

And so, Senator Cruz asked Jackson: "I also see a record of activism and advocacy as it concerns sexual predators that stems back decades, and that is concerning." Questions have meaning. Had Senator Cruz asked Judge Jackson whether she had ever written about Megan's Law, the question would have been neutral. But when you ask about *activism* and *advocacy* for sexual predators, then you mean what you say—that you are a person who is an activist and advocate for sexual predators. I've never met such a person.

Senator Cruz continued, "You wrote your note on the *Harvard Law Review* on sex crimes . . . Your note is entitled 'Prevention v. Punishment: Towards a principled distinction in the restraint of released sex offenders.' And in it, you argue, and I quote, "A recent spate of legislation purports to regulate released sex offenders by requiring them to register with local law enforcement officials, notify community members of their presence, undergo DNA testing, and submit to civil commitment for an indefinite term. Although many courts and commentators herald these laws as valid regulatory measures, others reject them as punitive enactments that violate the rights of individuals who have already been sanctioned for their crimes. Under existing doctrine, the constitutionality of sex offender statutes depends on their characterization as essentially preventative rather than punitive.' And what you go on to explain is that if they're viewed as punitive, they are unconstitutional."

Let me explain what Senator Cruz did not. Jackson's law school paper was an inquiry into the constitutionality of the components of Megan's Law and whether they were preventative (and hence likely constitutional) or punitive (hence likely unconstitutional). The paper argued that some of the components may well be characterized as punitive and, if so, risked being declared unconstitutional, while others were clearly preventative and would withstand constitutional scrutiny. None of that is tantamount to activism or advocacy on behalf of child predators. There is a great deal of legal scholarship and judicial writing on sentencing and the constitutionality of sentencing measures. Jackson was being neither incendiary, inflammatory nor particularly novel in considering the constitutionality of sentencing legislation. But the message that Senator Cruz was conveying to members of the public was clear.

Senator Cruz, undeterred by Judge Jackson's attempt to explain these legal issues, continued, "If the views you advocated for in law school prevailed, civil commitment laws across the country would be struck down, releasing sexual predators. And under the argument, community notification and DNA bank laws could well be struck down as well. Is that an outcome that should concern people?" And in another question: "If you look at civil commitment laws, the UCLA School of Law Williams Institute estimates more than 6,300 sex offenders are currently detained by civil commitment programs. . . . If the view you advocate prevailed, presumably, those 6,300 sex offenders would be released to the public. Is that an outcome that should be concerning?"

What is the question Senator Cruz asked? *Is that an outcome that should concern people*? The "outcome" he is referring to is releasing sexual predators. Let me rephrase what he asked: You are advocating for the release of 6,300 sexual predators into the community; is that something that people should be concerned about? And the answer is easy. Yes. Releasing sexual predators is something that "should concern people." But that is not what Ketanji Brown Jackson was saying in her law school paper, or as she tried to respond to the question. It is, however, precisely what Senator Cruz's carefully phrased question was designed to leave members of the public thinking.

Senator Cruz, you should know, was a Harvard colleague of the judge. He is legally educated. These questions were not asked to inform the public or engage in a legal discussion. The lawyer asking these questions knew precisely how to phrase them to achieve a particular goal, which was to give members of the public the impression that if Judge Jackson were left to her own devices, the country would be flooded with child predators.

Judge Jackson was further questioned about her law school days and her work as a young lawyer. She had submitted an amicus brief (Latin for "friend of the court") on behalf of Guantanamo Bay detainees who sought to challenge indefinite detention without trial. Senator Lindsey Graham was particularly chuffed about this. He asked whether she had argued that the United States could not hold enemy combatants indefinitely and that the government needed to try them or release them. Judge Jackson properly responded that her *clients* advanced that argument and it was her job to make the argument on behalf of her clients.

Undeterred, Senator Graham asked, "When you sign on to a brief, does it not become your argument?" Of course in an amicus brief it is never the lawyer's personal argument but rather the argument that the client wishes to advance. In amicus briefs, usually filed on behalf of public interest groups that are seeking to intervene in a case, the client has a specific position that they want advanced before the court. Senator Graham knows all of this. He is not only a lawyer by training but worked as a lawyer in the military.

The interchange continued:

Graham: You sign on to this brief making this argument, but you say it's not your position. I mean, why would you do that if it's not your position? Why would you take a client that has a position

like that? This is voluntary, nobody's making you
do this.

. . . If the court had taken the position argued
in the brief that you signed upon, it would have to
release these people or try them. . . . You're putting
America in an untenable position. This is not the way
you fight a war. If you try to do this in World War
Two, they'd run you out of town. . . .

Jackson: Respectfully, Senator, when you are an attorney and
you have clients who come to you, whether they pay
or not, you represent their positions before the court.

Graham: . . . I'm just trying to understand what made you
join this cause. You say somebody hired you, but
did you feel okay in *adopting* that cause? . . .

Jackson: Senator, as a judge now, in order to determine the
lawfulness or unlawfulness of any particular issue,
I need to receive briefs and information making
positions on all sides.

Graham: I got what a judge is all about. . . . I'm asking you to
explain a position you took as a lawyer regarding the
law of war. . . . If that brief had been accepted by the
court, it would be impossible for us to fight this war.

Again, trained lawyer Lindsey Graham knew exactly what
he was asking. In that question, he suggested Judge Jackson
fought for terrorists and that her advocacy was designed to
harm the United States.

It is impossible to fully capture the tenor of the room
during the confirmation hearing, but one moment more than
any other encapsulates it. In an outburst worthy of cartoon
rooster Foghorn Leghorn, a red-faced Senator Graham stormed

out of the Senate chamber after yelling in a southern drawl, "As long as they're dangerous, I hope they all die in jail if they're going to go back and kill Americans. It won't bother me one bit if thirty-nine of them die in prison. That's a better outcome than letting them go." He was talking about Guantanamo Bay detainees. The thing is, nobody was suggesting that the detainees should be let go to kill Americans. Ketanji Brown Jackson certainly was not.

She, in fact, quietly sat there, with barely a flicker of a reaction, as she did throughout much of the hearing. But, I figure, as a judge she'd presided over many uncontrollable people who are prone to histrionic displays. If Senator Graham were a woman, we would call her hysterical. But he's a man, and a senator at that, so I guess we can just call him self-righteously indignant. Although I swear, looking into his bulging eyes and sweaty brow on television, I could see the flicker of hysteria in his eyes. Poor man. If only he had understood the issue he was so upset about. Maybe he will take the time to read some cases about it so when he next addresses citizens of the United States, he can provide them with reasoned information instead of inflammatory questions and temper tantrums.

Most right-thinking people wouldn't want to release known terrorists from Guantanamo Bay, or anywhere else for that matter. But you see, some of the prisoners that were scooped up, we learned later, were not. Terrorists, that is. That's why trials are required—to figure out that precise thing. Who exactly was being held—indefinitely—in Guantanamo Bay? There are complex legal questions on both sides of this legal issue, such as society's interest in a public trial rather than a secret military one, and the ability to hold a public trial when much of the information the government would need to adduce is classified.

Legal minds most assuredly greater than Senator Graham's have grappled with these issues. In fact, the United States Supreme Court, in *Rasul v. Bush* (2004), *Hamdi v. Rumsfeld* (2004), *Hamdan v. Rumsfeld* (2006) and *Boumediene v. Bush* (2008), wrestled with these very questions and concluded that the government could not opt out of constitutional rights even in the no man's land of Guantanamo Bay. But I guess none of that occurred to Senator Graham. At least not when he was yelling.

Judge Jackson's record sentencing child pornographers was another significant point of attack. The senators focused on ten child pornography cases in her ten years on the trial bench. Senator Cruz must have spent a great deal of time putting together the demonstrative aid—large bristol boards setting out what the prosecutor had asked for, what the sentencing guidelines were, and what Judge Jackson had imposed as a sentence. Without exploring the specific facts of a single case, Cruz went down the list and pointed out that, on each occasion, Judge Jackson had imposed a sentence less than that requested by the prosecutor.

When Judge Jackson tried to explain that sentencing requires a judge to consider the offence, the victim and the offender, Cruz would have none of it. He asked: "Where the prosecutor asked for twenty-four months and you sentenced the offender to only three months, do you believe the voice of the child is heard?" The message that question was designed to convey is that in sentencing, Judge Jackson did not care about the victims.

The misleading nature of the question, which assumes facts to be true that are not, is precisely why judges caution juries that questions are not evidence.

In this case, many of the assumptions in Cruz's questions were not true. In five of the seven cases in which Judge Jackson imposed a lesser sentence than the sentencing guidelines recommendation, the sentence was consistent with or *higher than* the probation officer's recommendation. A probation officer's recommendation is accorded significant weight in an American court. And probation officers are not known for being soft on crime.

Two cases warrant particular mention. In *U.S. v. Hawkins* (2013), Judge Jackson imposed a sentence of three months' imprisonment and seventy-three months of supervised release in respect of one count of possession of child pornography. The sentence was lower than the probation officer's recommendation and lower than the government's request of twenty-four months' imprisonment. In her judgment, Jackson noted that the defendant possessed only thirty-three photos or videos, while the guidelines assumed possession of six hundred or more images. Importantly, he was only eighteen years old at the time of the offence, the images involved were of people not much younger than himself. He was a "model student and youth leader" who had received a scholarship to college and, crucially, the government had asked for a substantial downward departure from the guidelines. In other words, everyone involved in the case, from the prosecutor to the probation officer, was of the view that this was an exceptional case.

In *U.S. v. Chazin* (2021), Jackson imposed twenty-eight months of imprisonment and seventy-three months of supervised release. In explaining her departure from the sentencing guidelines, she noted that Chazin was twenty-five years old, had served in the military, had submitted numerous letters of support and had undergone a psychosexual evaluation by an expert who concluded he was not at increased risk of reoffending. Judge Jackson reviewed similar cases and concluded that her sentence was consistent with other precedents in her district and nationwide.

Sentencing is a complicated, highly individualized process. No two offenders are alike, and while courts attempt to maintain consistency in sentencing, they are also required to consider the individual being sentenced, the facts of the offence and the impact on the victim. Criminal punishment must deter the offender, deter other like-minded people and provide a measure of retribution and the opportunity for rehabilitation because we are, after all, a humane society that sees value in allowing people to re-enter society and become productive, pro-social members. Sentencing, if you polled judges, is one of the hardest parts of judging. It deserves a little more analysis than a bristol board can capture.

Judge Jackson, contrary to what Senator Cruz and his colleagues attempted to demonstrate, was not soft on crime, unaware of precedent or a novice to the complex considerations at play in sentencing. After all, for four years she had served on the United States Sentencing Commission, the government body that advises the federal government on matters of criminal sentencing. And the accepted view of the bar is that she was a judge who sentenced consistent with her colleagues. She was not an outlier or soft on crime.

But the misleading message the senators sought to convey in the questions they asked of her was that she was out of range in her sentencing and had a particular soft spot for child pornographers. Surely the senators did not expect members of the public to read up on the sentencing guidelines or when departures are appropriate, what Judge Jackson's sentences were like compared with those of other judges, the complexity of sentencing or the actual cases she was accused of improperly sentencing. The senators counted on most members of the public having neither the time nor the opportunity to delve deep into these legal issues. And so the questions, misleading as they were, could carry the day.

As one senator said, "I hope the American people can see through this sham. . . . God, I hate to say it because these have been my friends, but let me tell you, when it comes to this, you're looking for a fair process, you came to the wrong town at the wrong time, my friend." That was Senator Lindsey Graham exploding at the Democratic questioning of Supreme Court nominee Brett Kavanagh. Truer words have never been said. Too bad he forgot them.

Judge a man by his questions rather than his answers. All of these questions were asked by legislators, by the executive branch, by people who not only should defend core democratic values but should understand the role that an independent judiciary plays in upholding democracy. The disappointing theme in the Senate room was clear: Judge Jackson's work in criminal law, her work as a public defender, her work as an appellate lawyer filing amicus briefs on behalf of organizations that challenged laws, her work in sentencing in criminal cases—all of this was pointed to in order to demonstrate that she was morally bankrupt, that she sided with terrorists, that she was soft on child pornographers, that she endangered the welfare and safety of citizens.

The Eighth United Nations Congress on the Prevention of Crime and the Treatment of Offenders in 1990 adopted the Basic Principles on the Role of Lawyers. One principle specifically holds that "lawyers shall not be identified with their clients or their clients' causes as a result of discharging their functions." This was included precisely because the unique role that lawyers hold in the democratic architecture is understood, valued and a protected component of democracy. It is more than a little demoralizing to see this basic truth cavalierly ignored by American senators.

The questioning of Judge Jackson revealed the fissures in our democratic foundations and importantly who it is that carries at least some responsibility for the level of discourse among the public. If the very people elected to safeguard democratic values do not respect or understand the essential role that these judicial institutions have in protecting all citizens, if they are content to send misleading messages and yell fire in a theatre, then what chance do we have? The words of elected officials matter. Words can incite insurrections, foment distrust, create discord—or inform and educate.

When we wring our hands wondering why public discourse is devolving and why basic democratic values have now become points of contention and vigorous, even violent, disagreement, it is important to remember that the problem does not simply lie at the United States Senate door. In England, the influx of migrant workers has been a hot button issue for years. Members of Parliament have recently called lawyers and law firms amoral for representing such individuals in bringing challenges to the immigration laws. In 2020, a member of the public attempted to commit an act of violence at a law firm. Prosecutors alleged that the motivation was the firm's involvement in representing people facing deportation. But the accused had not come up with this idea all on his own. He had been handed it by government ministers. Days before, Home Secretary Priti Patel had tweeted that Home Office "removals continue to be frustrated by activist lawyers." Activist lawyers were blocking or delaying the removal of migrants.

Philip Rodney, a former member of the International Bar Association's Senior Lawyers' Committee Advisory Board, said, "I can't recall in more than forty years of practice seeing that sort of language being used by government in an attempt to discredit lawyers who are just doing their jobs." He said that it was "breath-taking that a government channel should seek to disparage as 'activists' lawyers who work within the limits of the law to uphold the rights of those whom they represent. The ability to scrutinize executive powers and protect the interests of our clients is an essential part of the rule of law." Undeterred, the home secretary gave a speech in which she denounced "lefty lawyers" working in the asylum system. She was supported by Prime Minister Boris Johnson, who accused "lefty human rights lawyers" of breaking the immigration system in the United Kingdom.

The result was that law firms working on immigration cases increasingly received threats from members of the public, so much so that the International Bar Association issued a statement saying, "We remind the United Kingdom of the UN Basic Principles' obligation for governments to 'ensure that lawyers are able to perform all of their professional functions without intimidation, hindrance, harassment or improper interference.'" The rhetoric was dangerous, even more so when the individuals spouting it were democratically elected officials. British lawyers who are challenging government sanctions against Russians in response to the Russian invasion of Ukraine have been "named and shamed" as being immoral by members of Parliament.

If you keep asking these types of misleading, wrongheaded questions, at some point you convince yourself that there is only one answer—or worse still, you convince the public to buy into a narrative that is false. You convince the public that the legal system, and the independence of lawyers and judges, exists to frustrate elected officials and is anti-democratic, when in truth it is part of the heart and soul of democracy. You warn the public about "activist" lawyers and "soft on crime" judges who will release a torrent of criminals and terrorists into society. You convince the public that the legal system and all its actors are corrupt. And when you have stripped one of the fundamental principles of our democracy, when you have crippled it, delegitimized it, called into question the moral integrity of those who work within it, what happens next?

You stop asking questions.

And this happens.

In 2021, in Russia, the opposition leader Alexei Navalny's lawyer, Ivan Pavlov, was arrested by the Russian Federal Security Service. A group of lawyers announced, "Ivan's arrest is connected to his professional activity. We believe that these actions by law enforcement are aimed exclusively at scaring Ivan and his colleagues in order to force them to reject an active position in defending their clients." And then, almost a year later, while Navalny's new lawyers, Olga Mikhailova and

Vadim Kobzev, were talking to journalists about his trial, they were arrested and driven away in a police bus.

First you ask the misleading question. You build a misleading narrative. You delegitimize and you sow distrust among the public. You solidify your power as being legitimate because you are elected and hence the voice of the people, and any institution that seeks to check or balance you is frustrating your legitimate objectives. And then you don't need to ask the question anymore. Because whoever is in power knows the answer that they want. You don't ask the question at all—you just arrest the lawyer, as happened in Russia, and happens in China, and in Iraq and Iran. You arrest the judges, as has happened in Pakistan.

Questions matter. Deliberately misleading questions asked by people who should know better, who are elected to know better, is attack on an institution created to stand outside the reach of politicians. If the executive branch of government does not understand what the roles of lawyers and judges are, if they do not want to protect core democratic values, if they are not the ones to champion it but instead denigrate it when it interferes with political ambitions, well, we are lost.

I'm happy that Judge Jackson has been confirmed. She is a qualified addition to the Supreme Court. But the broken road getting there—that will not be repaired by her appointment. Because those dangerous questions will forever hang in the air.

EPILOGUE

I AM NOT A CAT

BY THE TIME I'D finished this book, I'd passed fifty, dodged an embolic bullet, and then spent a lot of time over the next few years attending funerals for people who were far too young to die. This forced a begrudging acknowledgement that maybe, just maybe, I couldn't control everything. Apparently, rolling with life's punches was part of the deal. This tiny piece of wisdom resulted in a surprising sanguinity settling over me. I had just accepted this . . . and then the pandemic happened.

Looking back, it is our collective arrogance that still startles me the most. North Americans are blithely convinced that we are or should be generally immune from bad things happening to us. And to a larger extent, we have been justified in our blissful arrogance. Every once in a while, we experience a jolt. Think of the horror and shock over 9/11; the audacity that an act of war would come to our doorstep. It sent tremors through our self-indulgent systems. After all, the land of milk, and honey, and democracy, and freedom, through which we like to filter the North American story, could not possibly be so vulnerable. Going into other people's countries and flexing our muscles is generally considered our birth right. Not the other way round.

We obviously don't learn—2020 was a redux. Our heads were blithely up in the clouds or up somewhere else yet again. In January of 2020, we were hearing of a virus spreading through China and we watched with our usual detached interest at this foreign anomaly. It's as though we were driving by a car accident, only one that was happening thousands of miles away. Not for a second did it occur to us that the virus would have the gumption to cross the ocean and come to our shores. We were standing there watching the hurricane hurtle towards us and thinking how interesting the eye of the storm would look, not thinking we would be right in the midst of it. Or I did at least. Pandemic. Shmandemic. Much ado about nothing. It wouldn't—couldn't—level our house. But level it did.

I remember the week that it all happened. On Monday, March 9th, I had emailed my law partners and said maybe we should think about getting prepared in the event that we have to shut down our entire office. I started calling others in our profession and asked what, if anything, they were doing. Not much, it turned out. By Tuesday, the alert level had gone up. By Wednesday, we called an office meeting and asked our associates to contact their friends in the legal profession and find out what, if any plans, other firms had. And by 2:00 pm on Wednesday afternoon, we decided that we had to send everybody home. Courts shut down and were not prepared with the requisite technology for remote access to deal with the crisis that followed.

Like everyone, we did not emerge for over a year. Our life transformed over night to a virtual existence full of Zoom meetings, Zoom drinks, Zoom family gatherings, Zoom school, Zoom court, Zoom medical appointments. Human contact became a distant memory. A hug became a death wish.

I became chronically unrealistic and equally delusionally optimistic. For the first month, I was convinced that we would be done very shortly, a couple of weeks, maybe a month at most. By spring, the common view was that the pandemic would run into 2021 and I was convinced that we would be done by the summer and by summer, I knew we were in this for at least a year.

The justice system as we knew it came to a screeching halt, as did the practice of law as lawyers had known it throughout their lives. We migrated to Zoom hearings and trials from our home offices. Some of us were less tech savvy than others. In one case, a Texas lawyer joined a video court hearing using a Zoom filter that made him look like a fluffy white cat. While the two other lawyers were blasé as though cats routinely show up to make submissions, the judge started the hearing by gingerly commenting, "I *believe* you have a filter turned on in the video settings," as though it was possible, however remote, that a cat may in fact be practicing law. After some attempts to fix the glitch, the lawyer responded, "I'm ready to proceed. I'm here live judge. I am not a cat." The lawyer, astute that indeed there may be a cat somewhere in the United States practicing law during the pandemic, clarified that he is in fact a human. The video went viral.

And so it was with our Zoom practices. There were technical glitches, accidental filters, hearings often interrupted by dogs, children, or doorbells, people not knowing that we could see they were wearing a blazer with pajama pants (camera positioning is an art) and everyone attempting to adapt to litigation in a completely foreign context. I am not a cat, but I wasn't feeling particularly human either.

Within a week, I stopped watching the news. The daily death count made for good ratings but didn't help in understanding the virus, what the plan was for combatting it, what the science was behind it. It was too much to bear—the suffering of frontline workers, the vulnerability of the elderly, families struggling to figure out how to make it through. Everything.

I could not watch anymore and did the next most reasonable thing. I started trolling Tik Tok videos relating to dogs. I would wake up, grab my phone and start scrolling through. If I had a break, I would take a look at what new videos had been posted. I'm not gonna lie. I had my favorites. I didn't like the silly little dogs. Bull dogs were a raging favorite. My husband started doing the same thing. We would send them to each other (although we were in the same house) often sending the same ones. I grew alarmed that Trump was talking about banning Tik Tok. Why would he take such an outrageous position when there were so many cute dogs on it—even if it meant Tik Tok was tracking all my personal data and providing it to foreign nations. Giving up agency over all personal data was a small price to pay to see a bull dog in a funny costume. So I kept watching. And with each Tik Tok video, I lost one brain cell at a time. There was not a lot of distance between the bull dogs brain and mine. Clearly we were both enjoying the same things.

The truth is I wasn't doing so good. While I don't necessarily love the company of all people, I like my people, I like being in a crowd and I hate sitting with my own thoughts unnecessarily. My state was obvious to anyone who bothered to look through Zoom. I was giving up. You can often tell how I feel inside by how I'm doing on the outside. I have always asked my children to make one solemn promise—that no matter what life throws at them, they would never ever wear socks with sandals. My friend Laura, an ardent supporter of comfortable shoes and in particular, socks with Birkenstocks, always thought that my adamant refusal to even entertain the thought was misguided. Six months into the pandemic, after ordering every fluffy slipper I could find hoping that I could sink into them and drown my pandemic woes, I threw on a pair of socks . . . with sandals. There were days, to be honest, that I looked down at my comfortable feet and was ashamed that I had given up on life and with it the possibility that I could ever re-enter civilized society. But other days, I would send Laura photos of my latest socks and sandals combo with pride that I had finally had the internal fortitude to cross the treacherous Rubicon into the land of comfortable shoes.

And so it is with most moments of self-realization, unexpected and often small. Maybe all these years, my resistance to socks and sandals was just self-loathing. Was this what I had always wanted to do? Unleash my inner granola, give up frivolity and discomfort. Return to what is really important in life? Would it start at my feet and work its way through my whole being.

Once you have started, it is hard to stop. Discovering the new you. Why indeed stop at my feet, I asked. If this much joy could come with socks and sandals, was there more self-realization just around the corner? I had nowhere to go so I started reading "mindfulness" books, working on myself, tried meditating countless times, downloaded numerous apps, including one called "Calm" which did anything but calm me. And then I gave up. My pandemic self-journey wasn't all that fulfilling.

Many said that this pandemic had caused them to re-evaluate what was important—to reassess and recalibrate their lives. Those many of course were well-off folks. Was the pandemic really a time to reflect yet once again about ourselves? To turn inward yet again? To focus on how we could live a better life, be kinder to ourselves. Here is the truth: Most of the people that I know did just fine, lived in nice homes, and did not need to think about themselves even more. There was no need to change our lives, change course, and do more for ourselves. But out there, what I think you could not miss, is the fact that once again, any tragedy, any moment of misery is visited upon those who have the least to deal with it. So it is no surprise that the virus disproportionately nested in those communities and destroyed more racialized lives, more of the poor in North America and around the globe, than anyone else. It didn't find a good home in rich, white neighbourhoods probably because we were too busy cocooned in self-care, psychic growth and realization to let it in. Shielding many of us by all of this self-love, the virus was left to spread in more crowded, less self-indulgent neighbourhoods.

So when a friend asked me would I change my life after the pandemic, the answer was no, I will not. It was pretty good before, pretty good during, and will be pretty good after. I don't need *more* self-anything. Many others do. That is my pandemic realization.

So . . . I will not meditate. I will not become a yogi. I will not give up make-up and high heels. I'm not changing. Not even because of a pandemic. I am not going to become more inward facing. Because maybe, just maybe, the thing the pandemic was supposed to teach us is that lifting our noses from our own navels and looking out would be a little more valuable than looking in. For me at least. Self-care was not what was lacking.

The truth is bad things happen more to those that already bear more than their fair share of suffering. And yes, bad things even happen to some of us, all the way over here living the Dream in North America, even to the *Amrekani*, because guess what, we are not special.

I wish that I could tell you that I learned a great big post-pandemic lesson. I don't think I did. Well, maybe one.

Maybe, all those years ago, while my dad danced with such joy, I should've uncrossed my arms, looked up, and smiled, just a little bit. I'm gonna try. Look up and out and smile, just a bit more.

PHOTO CAPTIONS

1   My dad caught in mid-dance. His sheer joy annoying me as evidenced by my crossed arms.

5   With Mom and Dad in Beirut, Lebanon.

10   Gedo, Dad carrying me, Teta, and Sami visiting the caves in Lebanon. Second-hand smoke did not appear to be a concern for my dad, the pharmacist.

15   Mom, me, and Dad looking like very serious, respectable immigrants for our immigration application, although mom couldn't resist the wingtip black eyeliner.

20   Mom, Dad, and me celebrating my coronation in Vancouver.

27   Teta in a regal flowered chair in a wood paneled basement in Toronto.

31   Teta and Mom on Teta's suburban home veranda over-
      looking the ravine with Pete pondering where his
      clothes went.

40   The Caravan. One of our yearly Niagara Falls trips with
      my cousins.

49   Sami

53   The littlest four-year-old Drag Queen in town—after
      a dress-up session with Sami.

61   Sami and Teta in Europe, her one and only visit there.

72   Sami, stylish in a dapper white short suit while at a
      wedding of my Teta's sister in Jordan. Please note the
      knee extension—pre-Kim Kardashian Instagram-ready.

75   Mom on the beach in Alexandria, appropriately attired
      in leopard print capri pants.

77   Mom styling around Cairo and horse riding at the
      pyramids.

82   Mom and Sami in the botanical garden in Cairo in yet
      another handmade dress.

87   Mom and Dad at their engagement party, looking
      thrilled.

93   With Pete on Santa's lap just before we spontaneously

combust from polyester friction. Please note Pete's
excitement that Santa remembered to come back.

98   With Pete in a department store picture. Mullets were in.

105   Pete and I dressed up to present our fine art collection,
      courtesy of Honest Ed's department store in Toronto.
      We are flanking a Rococo-inspired baby porcelain
      Venus with scales.

107   With Pete posing with the bear I won at the exhibition
      and Pete took.

108   Dad with his first car in Canada, a Pontiac Parisienne,
      proudly posing in the snow. The picture was sent back
      to Cairo to demonstrate the North American miracle of
      snow and giant cars.

116   My dad and his parents, sister Renee, and two brothers
      (Labib and Saad). Dad has asked me to make sure that I
      point out that this picture was taken in Heliopolis,
      translated from Latin to mean City of the Sun.

119   My aunt Renee at eighteen-years-old.

120   With my cousin Hoda doing what we do best. . . eating.

127   With Eddie Greenspan.

131   My law school graduation photo. I would like to wear
      the cap to court one day. Just because.

140 With Marc Rosenberg at his Martin Criminal Justice Medal award ceremony.

155 The firm picture (as it then was). With my arms exposed. Well, one arm obviously exposed, which is less scandalous, I think.

171 With Mom and Dad celebrating the Law Society Medal award ceremony.

191 Me and a fake wolf, courtesy of the brilliant Matt Barnes.

215 Some of my girls celebrating my 50th. Danielle Robitaille, Heather Hansen, and Martha McCarthy looking more than hot, and me kinda hot . . . for 50.

227 Me kissing the oven for no apparent reason.

245 In Sami's NYC bathroom after dressing up, getting ready to go out to the Pyramid Club. I was sixteen-years-old.

ACKNOWLEDGEMENTS

THIS COULD NOT HAVE BEEN written without the privilege of the stories of my family. Thank you for letting me share a little bit of you. Most importantly, thanks to my parents who spent hours recounting their stories and digging through their memories for me. I hope it is the story that makes you proud. Mom, as usual, thank you for constantly brushing away any doubts or second thoughts I've had. You have cleared the way for me in more ways than you know.

To my friend Laura, thank you for hamster-wheeling with me, Bubbies, bubka, and all.

I am grateful to the supportive team at Penguin Random House Canada: Kristin Cochrane, Jared Bland, Kimberlee Hesas, Kelly Hill, and Erin Kelly, all of whom poured heart and soul into this, particularly Kristin and Jared who thought a lawyer's book without a law story would be just fine.

And of course to my editor and publisher, Doug Pepper, whose patience and no small amount of therapy guided this book and kept me sane in more ways than he knows. "Truth be told," I would not have been able to complete this book without his kindness and empathy.

And lastly, to my husband and two sons who have always been my greatest defenders, notwithstanding that I am frequently a difficult client.

MARIE HENEIN is a senior partner at Henein Hutchison LLP, recognized in *Canadian Lawyer* as one of the country's Top Ten Litigation Boutiques. She has been interviewed on CBC's *The National*, written for the *Globe and Mail*, and is a sought-after speaker. Named Toronto's 15th Most Powerful Person by *Toronto Life*, she has been repeatedly recognized as one of the Top 25 Most Influential Lawyers by *Canadian Lawyer* and was a recipient of the Laura Legge Award from the Law Society of Upper Canada and the Law Society of Upper Canada Medal. She lives in Toronto with her husband and two children.